OCR 9-1 GCSE Business

TARGET 9-5

Revision Handbook for Top Grades

Ian Marcousé

A-Z Business Training Ltd

Contents

Section 1: Business activity, marketing and people - Getting to Level 9

1.1 Enterprise and Entrepreneurship
- 1.1.1 The Purpose of Business and Enterprise 5
- 1.1.2 Characteristics of an Entrepreneur 6
- 1.1.3 The Concept of Risk and Reward 8

1.2 Business Planning
- 1.2.1 Business Plans 9
- 1.2.2 Importance and Usefulness of Business Plans 11

1.3 Business Ownership
- 1.3.1 Business Ownership and Liability 12
- 1.3.2 Suitability of ownership to context 14

1.4 Aims and Objectives
- 1.4.1 Business aims and objectives 15
- 1.4.2 Changes in Business Aims and Objectives 17

1.5 Stakeholders in Business
- 1.5.1 Stakeholders internal and external 18
- 1.5.2 Stakeholder effects to and from business 19

1.6 Business Growth
- 1.6.1 Organic growth 20
- 1.6.2 External growth – takeovers and mergers 21

Section 2

2.1 The role of marketing
- 2.1.1 The purpose of marketing within business 23
- 2.1.2 Understanding customer needs 24

2.2 Market research
- 2.2.1 Market research – purpose 25
- 2.2.2 Market research – methods and sources 26
- 2.2.3 Use and interpretation of market research 28

2.3 Market segmentation
- 2.3.1 Market segmentation 29

2.4 The Marketing Mix
- 2.4.1 Introduction to marketing mix 30
- 2.4.2 Product (including product life cycle) 32
- 2.4.3 Price 34
- 2.4.4 Promotion 36
- 2.4.5 Place 37

2.4.6	Marketing Mix and Decisions	38
2.4.7	Interpretation of market data	40

Section 3

3.1	**The Role of Human Resources**	
3.1.1	Purpose of Human Resources	41
3.2	**2 Organisation structure**	
3.2.1	Identifying and meeting human resource needs	42
3.2.2	Terminology of organisation charts	43
3.2.3	Different ways of working	44
3.3	**Communication in Business**	
3.3.1	Communications	45
3.4	**Recruitment and Selection**	
3.4.1	Effective recruitment	46
3.4.2	Methods of selection	47
3.5	**Motivation and Retention**	
3.5.1	Importance of Employee Motivation	48
3.5.2	Financial and non-financial methods of motivation	50
3.5.3	Importance of employee retention	51
3.6	**Training & development**	
3.6.1	Importance of Employee Motivation	52
3.6.2	Why business train their workers	54
3.7	**Employment law**	
3.7.1	Impact of legislation on recruitment and employment	55

Section 4

4.1	**Production Processes**	
4.1.1	Production Processes	56
4.1.2	Technology and production	58
4.2	**Quality of goods and services**	
4.2.1	Quality management	59
4.3	**Sales process and customer service**	
4.3.1	The sales process	60
4.3.2	Customer service and engagement	62
4.4	**Consumer law**	
4.4.1	Impact of consumer law on business	63
4.5	**Business Location**	
4.5.1	Factors affecting business location	64

4.6	**Working with suppliers**	
4.6.1	Procurement	65

Section 5

5.1	**Role of finance function**	
5.1.1	Purpose and influence of finance function	66
5.2	**Sources of finance**	
5.2.1	Reasons business need finance	67
5.2.2	Suitable finance	68
5.3	**Revenue, costs, profit and loss**	
5.3.1	Revenue and costs	70
5.3.2	Profit and loss	72
5.3.3	Calculating profitability and Average rate of return	74
5.4	**Break-even**	
5.4.1	Break-even	76
5.5	**Cash and cash flow**	
5.5.1	Cash and cash flow	78

Section 6

6.1	**Ethical and environmental considerations**	
6.1.1	Ethics and Environment in business	80
6.2	**The economic climate**	
6.2.1	The economy and business	82
6.3	**Globalisation**	
6.3.1	Business and Globalisation	83
6.3.2	How businesses compete internationally	84

Section 7

7	**Interdependent nature of business**	
7.1	Business and Globalisation	85
7.2	How businesses compete internationally	86
7.3	Impact of risk and reward on business activity	87
7.4	Use of financial information in understanding performance	88

Section 8

8.1	Application: the Key Skill	89
8.2	Answers to Maths Questions	90

The Purpose of Business Activity and Enterprise

What? (Grade 5 basics)

There are three possible purposes of business activity: to make money, to satisfy the needs of customers or to aim for a higher purpose, such as to bring the world closer together (an early goal for Google). To achieve any or all of them, the first requirement is to spot an opportunity. Then that opportunity must be developed into an idea for a sustainedly profitable business.

Why? (Grade 6)

However ambitious the social or moral goals, no business can last long without money to pay the wages and the bills. So there has to be a way to turn the opportunity into something that can generate enough revenue to cover the day-to-day costs. Plus – ideally – enough extra (the profit) to pay for new investments or new developments. No business can last long without money being spent on improving its look and its effectiveness.

How? (Grade 7)

The best way to achieve sustained profitability is to understand how to handle different businesses in different circumstances. Chocolate sales in the UK have been around £3,000 million a year for a decade; new brands come and go; campaigners for better health come and won't go; but chocolate remains an amazingly stable market in the UK. By comparison, the market for bicycles has been a sensation. Sales of bikes for adults have nearly doubled in the past ten years, with dramatic increases in sales of £1,000 bikes (and electric bikes to come). Clever businesspeople see the need to act differently in different markets.

So? (Grade 8)

Although every business needs profit to survive and thrive, not every entrepreneur sees profit as the purpose (or goal). In a small town, someone might start up a small football club because they love the game (and their son's a pretty good player). Years' later that club might gain promotion to the football league. That's success, whether or not there was enough profit to pay out dividends.

Grade 9

Your examiners love to see business methods used for social purposes, such as a recycling business or one focused on electric cars. Of course, most businesses are focused mainly on profits and therefore dividends to shareholders. But a large number of exam questions feature businesses with a higher social purpose.

> **Do** think about the purpose of the business featured in the exam paper. The purpose of a family business such as a farm may mainly be to keep the family together. So say so

> **Don't** ignore the fact that some businesses have no real purpose. The High Street's seventh betting shop has no social purpose (in fact it's a social evil) and may not even prove profitable. Here's hoping.

> **Exam tip:** remember that profit has two purposes: to finance the growth of the business – and to make the owners rich – everyone would see the first purpose as a good thing

---

Purpose of business: 5-step logic chain (to get to the top response level)

Chain 1. All businesses want to survive, so a change in technology can cause a problem (1) forcing the business to respond to rivals (2) … though if they haven't kept up with their R&D spending they may be too far behind to catch up (3) … leaving them to cut costs to try to survive (4) … which may only make their problems worse, for example if they cut advertising and branding support (5)

Chain 2. If the purpose is to satisfy customer needs the enterprise should be off to a great start (1) … making good use of quantitative and qualitative market research (2) and being willing to change things in line with customer tastes (3). It's important to realise that the opportunity the business spotted may change subtly (4) … but if customers change, so too must the business. (5)

Characteristics of an Entrepreneur

What? (Grade 5 basics)

Entrepreneurship is the set of skills and attitudes that enable some people to put into practice ideas that others only dream about. Key characteristics of an entrepreneur include confidence and creativity, enjoying risk-taking, showing resilience (bounce-back-ability) and having a steely determination.

Why? (Grade 6)

Entrepreneurs set themselves apart by an optimistic outlook that makes them focus more on opportunities than threats. They usually find risk-taking exciting rather than scary. Perhaps it comes in part from curiosity, as in 'I wonder whether …?' So why do they do it that way? Because they love a challenge, are attracted to risk and have the confidence to go right ahead.

How? (Grade 7)

Some entrepreneurs stumble on the thing that makes them rich, such as Mark Zuckerberg at Facebook. Others look at a growing market and use their creativity to find their own, successful place within it. Six years after ASOS began, Mahmud Kamani and Carol Kane founded Boohoo.com, another UK online fashion site. By its 10th birthday Boohoo was making £30 million profit a year. Some start up with pennies in the bank; others have wealthy families behind them. There are as many possibilities as there are start-ups.

So? (Grade 8)

When judging a start-up story featured in an exam, look not only at whether it went well but also at the circumstances of the entrepreneur. There is something especially impressive about those who started up with little or no money. Some will have risked their life savings (impressive) and some go further and risk the family house and stability (reckless!).

Grade 9

Grade 9 students see how concepts link together, such as entrepreneurship and risk/reward. They also see that creativity and risk-taking mean nothing unless the business is focused on satisfying the needs of customers. These skills makes it much easier to construct a well-developed answer to the bigger, 9-mark evaluate questions. And these are the questions that swing the grades.

Do think about the whether the entrepreneur has the right characteristics for start-up. Many have the ambition and the desire to be their own boss, but lack the drive and determination

Don't be too hard on an entrepreneur who's struggling at the start. There are so many balls to juggle that it's understandable if some drop to the floor.

Exam tip: keep a strong focus on the circumstances of the start-up, such as the actions of competitors and whether the business is really meeting customer wants.

Entrepreneurship: 5-step logic chain (to get to the top response level)

Chain 1. Most entrepreneurs seek to run a profitable business (1) … based on meeting customer needs (2). As every market is competitive, this needs a clever idea or a clever way to implement a standard idea (3). It is easy to think entrepreneurship is all about clever ideas and risk-taking (4), but it's also about organising resources to meet or beat customer needs and expectations (5).

Chain 2. A good entrepreneur takes an innovative idea (1) … that's focused on customer needs (2) … then raises the cash (3) to turn the idea into a great customer experience (4) … that keeps people coming back and encourages others to come and try (5).

Answering exams

OCR produces sample exam papers to help teachers. In these there are several questions about entrepreneurs. There are also broader questions in which a paragraph on enterprise would be very useful. Here are two questions of value, the second is based on OCR's specimen exam paper 1, 'Shirtz Ltd'.

1. State two characteristics of an entrepreneur. (2 marks)

2. Evaluate whether Shamira and Zubair should rent a new location now, or wait for the business to grow. (9 marks)

On the right are strong answers to these two questions. They focus on how entrepreneurship can be used in the answers – and the answer to Q2. is a high-mark answer to a 9 mark question.

Grade 9 Answers (Qs. on the left)

1.
- *A risk-taker*
- *Creative approach to problem solving*

2. Shamira and Zubair (S&Z) have set out clearly the objective of renting a new location. Probably they have found too many disadvantages to having the business based in a room in their house. These may be family-based (kids demanding separate rooms) or may be to do with the efficiency of the business. The text says they need new machinery which might be too big for the room in their house.

S&Z must think things through with care. If they are currently unable to keep up with customer demand because of limits on space, there's a strong case for moving to new premises – especially if they have checked their finances and know that this is affordable.

The biggest concern about their plan, though, is that they don't seem to have worked out how much new finance they are going to need, nor where to get it from.

On balance S&Z must beware of expanding just because they want to get out of the house. Production expansion is fine, but only if there's enough customer demand – and there's enough money to finance the expansion.

Further Exam tip. GCSE examiners love stories about new business start-ups, so the short business cases used in the exam will often be based on start-up (and therefore entrepreneurship).

Help prepare yourself for this by taking some interest in the start-up process, from Youtube clips of Dragon's Den on BBC TV to re-reading the many cases of start-up your teachers will have used in class. Also, a useful (and free) online resource is www.startups.co.uk which has a super section on 'How They Started'.

The Concept of Risk and Reward

What? (Grade 5 basics)

Risk is the possibility that things will go wrong. It can be quantified, as in: 'there's only a 30% chance of success' and therefore a 70% chance of failure. Poor outcomes can lead to financial losses, lack of security or even the outright failure of a business.

Reward comes from the benefits of success. This might be in the form of profit - or from personal independence for the entrepreneur whose success provides control over his/her life.

> **Do** think about the risks involved for that specific entrepreneur: has a family? Wealthy enough to take a loss?

Why? (Grade 6)

Entrepreneurs make decisions by weighing up risks compared with rewards. It might be worth taking a big risk if there's a possibility of a huge reward. In 2016 Skyscanner – a £100 start-up by 3 Scottish university students in 2001 – was bought for £1,400 million. So the reason why risk-reward matters is because it's a fundamental part of businesspeople's decision-making.

How? (Grade 7)

To judge risk against reward, you first need a numerical estimate of the level of risk. In the UK fewer than 1 in 5 new products becomes a success, so the risk of failure is 4 out of 5 (80%). But in a market such as healthy snacks, the reward for success can be sales of £20 million a year (Nakd cereal bars). So reward can be weighed against risk.

> **Don't** be too inclined to avoid risk; business decisions are about the future, so every decision carries risk. Risk is not a bad thing; it's a fact of business life.

So? (Grade 8)

In the exam, never treat risk as a problem. In business risk is a factor to set against reward to make a judgement about whether or not to go ahead. All decisions are about the future, which introduces an element of risk. But as long as the rewards are good enough, risks are worth taking.

Grade 9

Risk has an ethical element as well. Me risking my money is my problem. But me risking other people's money may be their problem. An under-financed start-up may collapse at the cost of blameless customers and suppliers. They probably didn't realised the risks they were being encouraged to take. Good entrepreneurs take risk upon themselves; 'cowboys' impose risk on others.

> **Exam tip**: it's easy to focus too much on risk (the downside). Balance your argument by writing clearly about reward as well.

Risk & Reward: 5-step logic chain (necessary to get to the top response level)

Chain 1. Both risk and reward can be measured or estimated (1) ... so they can be balanced against each other (2) ... which allows those with lots of capital to take big risks as long as the rewards are even bigger (3) . Businesspeople with less capital may accept that this risk is not for them (4) ... because they can't afford the losses involved if the idea fails (5)

Chain 2. Risk is caused by ignorance of customer wants. Nokia bet on buttons but the market wanted Apple's touchscreen. (1) ... To measure risk (and reward) market research is needed (2). This may lead to better decisions, which reduces risk (3) ... and may boost the levels of rewards available (4) which helps the business finance better long-term developments (5)

Business plans

What? (Grade 5 basics)

First-time entrepreneurs face a struggle to bring together all the financial, marketing, production and human aspects of running a business. A business plan is a way to cope with this problem. It's a document that sets out the business aims and objectives plus all the financial and other plans for how to achieve them.

Why? (Grade 6)

For new and experienced entrepreneurs alike, a business plan is a valuable document for gaining external finance. Bankers want to see your plan to help them judge the risks involved in the business proposition. While for banks the key thing is risk, for potential investors in the company's shares, at least as important are the potential rewards. Venture capital investors are looking for 'scalability' – the ability of the small business idea to be expanded into something huge – and hugely profitable.

How? (Grade 7)

Writing a business plan starts with the opportunity you have identified. Perhaps your town has only one, pricey but second-rate, Thai restaurant. And you're sure you can do better. Then you need some market research, a forecast of weekly revenues and – most important of all – a cash flow forecast. Other decisions can then be added in such as the planned location, the planned marketing mix and the desired sources of finance.

So? (Grade 8)

Any entrepreneur who seeks outside investors or lenders needs a business plan. But they may find the plan far more useful still. Once funding is sorted and it's time for action, the business plan helps provide a week-by-week guide for what to do, how to do it and the maximum that can be spent. For first-time entrepreneurs especially, the plan can become their business bible.

Grade 9

The secret to success with a business plan is to be doubly careful: to estimate your revenues and cash inflows on the low side, and cash outflows on the high side. And then show even more caution by making a generous allowance for 'contingencies' - things that shouldn't go wrong, but might. Bankers will be particularly impressed by a plan that shows understanding that starting a business is hard – so plenty of spare cash should be built into the plan.

> **Do** show the examiner you understand how difficult business planning must be for a first-time entrepreneur. The more knowledge and experience of the industry, the better the chances of success

> **Don't** focus too much on profit in the early stages of a new business. Cash is King.

> **Exam tip:** for a 6, 9 or 12-mark question, focus your answer on the key parts of the business plan: the idea, the market research and the cash flow forecast. Don't end up listing lots of different elements of the plan.

Business plans: 5-step logic chain (getting to the top response level)

Chain 1. For a young, first-time entrepreneur bankers and investors will pick holes in the plan (1) ... so it will need to be exceptionally well researched (2) ... especially in the forecasts of sales and cash flow (3). It would help to have the plan checked thoroughly by an older mentor (4) ... who could come along to meetings with bankers and investors – to reassure them that the idea has legs. (5)

Chain 2. If an entrepreneur has already succeeded with Shop Number 1, it's tempting to rush the business plan for shop 2 (1) ... but actually there's a great opportunity here (2) ... a careful plan for Shop 2 would analyse why Shop 1 succeeded (3) ... and how its success can be reproduced (4). This might encourage investors to put a lot of capital into the business, to finance rapid growth. (5)

Answering exams

OCR produces sample exam papers to help teachers. In these there is only one question directly about business plans. But in the Board's marking guidance there are plenty of mentions of business plans, or elements within the plan. So it is an area that helps in answering many different questions.

Here are 3 questions where business plans are a significant part of the answer:

1. Explain one reason why an entrepreneur would produce a business plan. (2 marks)

Q2. Analyse one disadvantage to an entrepreneur of sticking too rigidly to their start-up business plan. (3 marks)

The third question is based on a start-up of a business called Shirtz Ltd (see OCR's Specimen Paper 1)

Q3. Evaluate the effectiveness of Shirtz Ltd's business plan. (9 marks)

On the right are strong answers to these three questions. They focus on how a business plan can be used in the answers. They are models for using the plan rather than models for how to score 9 or 12 marks.

Grade 9 Answers (see questions on the left)

1. One reason is if the entrepreneur is hoping to take out a bank loan. The bank wants evidence that their capital is safe because the business plan is well-researched and the cash flows estimated with caution.

2. A start-up business plan is written before the business has started. No-one would expect it to be exactly right about weekly revenues or monthly cash flows. When things turn out differently than expected, a good entrepreneur will make changes, such as acting to cut costs if sales are proving a disappointment. Sticking rigidly to the plan would be unbusinesslike.

3. Most business plans are produced for external funders such as banks or venture capital investors. As 'new finance' will be required to get Shirtz towards its growth objective, a main criticism must be that it lacks the detail needed to get investors to invest. There are no forecasts of future cash flows or profits – and not even a figure for the amount needed to achieve the aims and objectives.

On the other hand it could be said to be a coherent plan for meeting growth objectives. New resources such as machinery and premises are identified, together with new full-time staff and a plan for changes to the marketing mix. The lack of detail is unnerving, but Shamira and Zubair have appreciated that growth means new plans are required for every section of the business – not just finance.

Overall, though, unless they can provide far greater detail (especially numbers such as sales, revenue and profit forecasts) Shamira and Zubair are likely to be turned down when asking for new finance.

Role and importance of a business plan

What? (Grade 5 basics)

A business plan sets out the business aims and objectives plus the financial, marketing and other plans for how to achieve them. The role is to map out the actions that can turn an idea into a business success. The importance is that entrepreneurs face a huge number of different challenges. This can be overwhelming. The business plan is a reminder of what was supposed to happen – and when. So it's useful in helping to avoid panic.

Why? (Grade 6)

An easy mistake to make is to chase sales. If sales are slow in week one at a new café, it's tempting to put posters up offering special deals to customers. But if you'd identified that your market would be busy, health-conscious office-workers, it may be best to wait. Price-cutting risks damaging your message to the market you've identified. Instead of 'Oh, that's the café with good, healthy food', it becomes 'Oh, that's the bargain-basement place'. Best to stick with your business plan.

How? (Grade 7)

The key is to identify the resources the business needs to operate effectively, such as the right equipment, fully-trained staff – and enough capital to get beyond the early, loss-making period. When set out clearly on the business plan the entrepreneur should know what to buy and who to hire – and by when.

So? (Grade 8)

Many entrepreneurs are financing their first business using their own – or their family's – life savings. So they have a duty to do all they can to minimise the risks involved. And that includes drawing up a detailed business plan. The more detail there is in the plan the more likely it is to be a success.

Grade 9

The perfect plan guides the business towards achieving its aims and objectives. It would do this in a way that turns a business idea into a detailed plan of action that has the flexibility to deal with different issues and problems. For example it has built in a sufficient financial reserve (cushion) to mean that one month of dreadful weather cannot prevent the business from succeeding.

> **Do** show the twin benefits of a business plan: good for getting external finance but also helpful in turning a good idea into a good outcome.

> **Don't** make it seem that the plan is unchangeable. Flexibility is a huge quality in a good plan. No-one knows what will happen in the future, so a plan may have to be adapted to new circumstances.

> **Exam tip:** at the heart of every good business plan is a carefully considered cash flow forecast. Examiners know that this is at the heart of a good plan.

Business planning: 5-step logic chain (getting to the top response level)

Chain 1. A good plan starts by identifying the market opportunity or gap (1) … then builds the business around the gap, e.g. hiring and training staff to deal with older but richer customers (2) … then organises other resources such as marketing and operations (3) … to make sure that a bright idea (4) … can be turned into a sustainable competitive advantage. (5)

Chain 2. Plans usually start with aims and objectives (1) … then develop a plan around what's needed to succeed with them. (2) This may require heavy investment into marketing and people (3) … which will be fine as long as the finances are available (4). Strong teams of venture capital investors can be hugely helpful in this. (5)

Business Ownership

What? (Grade 5 basics)

There are two types of business: those with limited liability and those with unlimited liability. If an entrepreneur hires a market stall and starts trading, this type of business is called a 'sole trader' and it has unlimited liability. This means any losses or debts created by the business remain the personal responsibility of the owner – that entrepreneur. Only by forming a company do the shareholder/owners enjoy limited liability.

Why? (Grade 6)

The reason 'limited liability' was introduced in the UK was to encourage entrepreneurs by reducing the risks to themselves and their families. You can invest your life savings – and potentially lose every penny – but with limited liability you can't be liable for any more than the sum you've invested. So banks can't come after your own money, or house, or car. With unlimited liability they can.

How? (Grade 7)

To get the protection of limited liability you form a company. To do this you need nothing more than proof of identity and to pay a fee of around £60. Private limited companies are small family businesses that say Ltd after the business name, e.g. Spartex Ltd. A public limited company needs considerably more capital, must meet tougher financial rules, but has the opportunity to be listed on the stock market.

So? (Grade 8)

The owners of unlimited liability businesses such as sole traders and partnerships must be extra careful to avoid losses. This may mean they hardly ever go on holiday, because they are too worried about leaving the business in a stranger's hands. The sole trader is unlimitedly liable, so a mistake made by friend trying to look after the business could damage the entrepreneur's personal finances.

Grade 9

By law, every limited liability business must announce its status by showing Ltd or Plc (Public limited company) after its name. This warns others of the risks in dealing with the company. Perhaps the business will close down after running out of cash - and as the owners have limited liability, they don't need to pay the debts. So it's riskier to lend money to a limited company than to an unlimited business.

Do decide on your business organisation early on in the process. A private company suits a small family business with a relatively high risk business idea

Don't forget that partnerships have unlimited liability. If one partner makes a dreadful mistake, costing thousands, all other partners will be equally liable financially. If you're a partner, you can suffer from other people's mistakes.

Exam tip: look to see if the business name has Ltd or Plc after it. If not, the business has unlimited liability. And therefore is a big risk for the proprietor.

Options for Business Ownership: 5-step logic chain (to get the top response)

Chain 1. Most new UK businesses start up as sole traders or partnerships (1) … meaning that they have unlimited liability (2) … this seems unnecessarily risky (3) … but it may be that the financial risks are too low to worry about (4) … such as starting a new online business in which failure would mean a waste of man-hours, but little risk of serious financial losses (5)

Chain 2. For a new business with serious growth prospects a private limited company structure is ideal (1) … because it's easy to bring new investors in by selling them shares in the business (2) … with no risk of further losses if the business fails (3). But the disadvantage is sharing future profits with your new shareholders (4) … who may also want a say in the main business decisions to be taken by the founder (5)

Answering exams

Of all the topics on the course, none is examined as regularly as this. I can virtually guarantee one or more direct questions on limited/unlimited liability or sole trader/partnership/private limited companies. Business ownership can also be used to analyse many business situations and answer many high-mark questions, such as the 6-mark Q18a) on the OCR specimen paper (see Q2 below, and www.ocr.com)

Here are three questions in which the options for start-up can be a significant part of the answer. The first two are based on OCR's specimen papers.

Q1. Explain one disadvantage to a sole trader of having unlimited liability. (2 marks)

Q2. Analyse two benefits to Shamira and Zubair of Shirtz Ltd being a private limited company. (6 marks)

Q3. Discuss whether a new business would be better off starting out as a sole trader or a partnership. (6 marks)

On the right are strong answers to these three questions. They show the importance of understanding business ownership – and also show the need to have thorough understanding of every aspect of this topic.

With some topics it's possible that there will be no questions on *your* exam. Not in this case. Options for start-up will be there.

Grade 9 Answers (questions on left)

Q1. *For a sole trader the business is legally no different from the person. Personal liability is unlimited. So if the business loses money, its debts must be repaid by the individual owner.*

Q2.

Benefit 1. The text mentions their house, and a clear benefit of an Ltd structure to Shamira and Zubair is that – even if the business makes serious losses – no-one can make a claim on their personal property. Their business liabilities are limited to the money they put in to the business.#

Benefit 2. The text says they need 'new finance' for their expansion plan. Having a private company structure means they can sell shares to friends and family – bringing share capital into the business without risking losing voting control.

Q3) The great strength of a sole trader is the clarity that one person is in charge – and that same person takes 100% of the profits – and 100% of any losses. On the other hand it's tough to get away on holiday, because it's hard to trust any 'business babysitter' when any mistake affects the unlimited liability of the sole trader.

A partnership has benefits, both by expanding the possible investment of capital (2+ investors rather than one) and by sharing responsibility. Going on holiday shouldn't be a problem. But entrepreneurs typically love to be in control – it's one of the great appeals of starting on your own – so it's very hard to share decision making. The risk is of arguments and disagreements that may tear the business apart.

On balance, it's only sensible to go into partnership if you know the partner well enough to be able to argue – scream, even – but still be on speaking terms tomorrow.

Section 1.3: Business Ownership

Suitability of ownership to context

What? (Grade 5 basics)

There are far more unlimited liability businesses in the UK than limited liability (companies). And most are sole traders. So this form of ownership must be much more suitable than you might think. After all, it seems obvious for a business owner to opt for the security offered by limited liability. Therefore you expect there to be lots of private limited companies. But there are twice as many unlimited liability businesses (sole traders and partnerships) as limited ones (private and public companies).

Why? (Grade 6)

Three quarters of all UK businesses have no employees. In other words the business is simply the owner, e.g. a plumber who trades under the name *Harrogate Plumbers*. For such a small business there may be few financial risks to worry about – therefore the entrepreneur stays as a sole trader. This avoids the paperwork and annual accounting required for all (limited) companies.

How? (Grade 7)

To match the type of ownership to the business context there two key tests: does the business use a lot of credit and or borrow a lot from banks? If so, a limited liability structure makes a lot of sense. It protects the owner from any possible debts run up by the business. And secondly, just how profitable may your business prove to be? Annual accounts have to be published for limited companies, but not for sole traders or partnerships. So if you want to hide your huge profits from the eyes of others, stay as a sole trader.

So? (Grade 8)

Ambitious entrepreneurs hoping to float their companies and make £hundreds of millions would be wise to start up as a private limited company, then develop towards public (plc) status. Only those with modest financial objectives should consider sole trader or partnership status.

Grade 9

Although it's clear that some businesses should become companies, it's less clear why any businessperson would want to be in a partnership. This structure allows you to not only lose personal capital due to your own mistakes, but also due to mistakes by your partner(s). Most regard it as a structure that's never suitable.

> **Do** think hard about when sole trader status might be best – including for a low-cost start-up which is short of capital – better, perhaps, to avoid higher accountants' fees for a limited company

> **Don't** underestimate the downsides of becoming a public limited company (plc). Ownership and control are under permanent threat from outside shareholders, who also may encourage the business to focus too much on the short term

> **Exam tip**: remember that a private company has limited liability – always. That might make suppliers reluctant to supply on credit- as they know the owners can walk away without paying

---

Suitability of Ownership: 5-step logic chain (to get the top response)

Chain 1. Some businesses inevitably require borrowing, such as housebuilding companies (1) …They can't ask for cash before the house exists, so borrowing is needed (2). This makes a limited liability structure especially important (3) … but in other cases you might see that a sole trader or partnership approach should work better (4) … If so, explain why with confidence. (5)

Chain 2. For a fast growing business a public limited company structure can work well (1) … as a flotation can raise huge sums by selling shares to new investors (2) … and avoid raising capital by large-scale borrowing from the bank (3). But the disadvantage is sharing future profits with your new shareholders (4) … who also have a say in future business decisions. (5)

Aims and Objectives

What? (Grade 5 basics)

Business aims and objectives are the goals and targets that the owners wish to achieve. They can be divided into:

- financial targets such as survival, profit, growth and market share
- and non-financial targets such as providing a service, personal satisfaction and independence

Why? (Grade 6)

There are so many different pressures affecting a business at any one time that it's helpful if all staff know where the business is supposed to be heading. Managing a football team is easy: 3 points this Saturday please, and a trophy by May. Most businesses are much more complicated so clear aims and objectives provide a clear sense of direction which, in turn, helps in decision-making.

How? (Grade 7)

Anyone who starts their own business has personal objectives that may never be written down. A common non-financial one is to 'be your own boss'; at the start, most entrepreneurs are just looking for survival. Once things have settled down, the financial objectives will change towards market share and profit. Later there may be a change to growth as the entrepreneur starts to enjoy business success

So? (Grade 8)

Different aims lead to different business decisions. A family-owned business aiming for long-term financial security (such as BMW) might invest for the future, taking care to avoid selling poor quality goods that might damage the brand/family name. Whereas a business aiming for maximum short-term profit might cut corners in order to boost this year's earnings. And a business started by an entrepreneur seeking 'a challenge' might take a few too many risks.

Grade 9

At the top level it's good to know the difference between aims and objectives. An aim is a general statement of where the business should be heading. An objective is much more specific, perhaps even SMART: Specific, Measurable, Achievable, Realistic, Time-bound. Aim: Profit Growth. Objective: boost profit by 25% this year and 50% within 3 years.

> **Do** be clear that aims and objectives are the drivers of business decisions, e.g. deciding whether to launch a new product or to squeeze more profit out of existing ones.

> **Don't** assume that businesses always set the right objectives. Tesco once set the objective of growth and ended up in a disastrous expansion into the USA. It cost £2 billion in losses.

> **Exam tip**: examiners are particularly interested in social objectives, e.g. setting up a business to provide a service, such as a Food Bank. But even charitable businesses need profits to keep going and growing.

Aims and Objectives: 5-step logic chain (to get to the top response level)

Chain 1. Aims and objectives are at the heart of a start-up business plan (1) ... as they set out the targets for the first few years (2) ... perhaps including SMART targets (3) ... that show the precise profit target for Year 1 and the finance required to get there (4). Without clear aims and objectives it would be hard – perhaps impossible – to get any outsider to invest in your new business. (5)

Chain 2. Aims and objectives differ between businesses because they are based on circumstances, competition and individual preferences (1) ... so one business tries to maximise market share (think Samsung) while another wants long-term financial security (2) ... in order to hand over the business to the next generation (3) ... perhaps with a reputation for quality and integrity (4) to reflect well on the family name (5)

Answering exams

Aims and objectives will frequently be tested in the Paper 1 exam, and may also be an important part of Paper 2 answers. Here are 3 questions where aims and objectives are at the heart of things:

Q1. Explain one benefit to a business of having clear aims and objectives. (2 marks)

P2 Explain how Boohoo's objectives may have changed since 2006. (2 marks)

Q3. Discuss whether it is possible for a business to succeed if the owner/partners have different aims and objectives for the business. (6 marks)

On the right are strong answers to these three questions. They focus on how aims and objectives can be used in the answers – so they are models for using this topic rather than models for how to score 6 marks.

Extra Exam Tip:

Entrepreneurs often have a personal objective of 'being their own boss'. In fact running a small business can soon feel like you have many bosses, from customers to big, powerful suppliers. So be alert to when an owner's non-financial aims and objectives prove hard to achieve in reality.

Grade 9 Answers (see questions on the left)

Q1 Clear aims and objectives matter when a business starts taking on extra staff. Everyone needs to know the targets the business has for the future. This makes it easier to make the right choice when staff are faced with tricky decisions.

Q2. When Boohoo started up in 2006 its two founders may have thought of little else than surviving in the fiercely competitive online market for clothing. Today it's fully established and may have the objective of gaining market share from rival ASOS.

Q3. If one boss wants high profits while the other is focused on social objectives, the business has a problem. The two bosses will make different decisions when faced with similar problems or customer queries. That will be confusing for staff who won't know the 'right' thing to do when faced with a similar situation.

Despite this, it must still be possible for the business to succeed if it's fortunate enough to be in the right place at the right time. The launch of Green & Black's organic chocolate was full of problems between the two founders – yet Cadbury bought the business for £50 million. Surely that's success.

So although a failure to agree aims and objectives is a huge handicap, it is still possible for the business to be a success.

Changes in Aims and Objectives

What? (Grade 5 basics)

The aims and objectives of a business are likely to change as a business develops. From a focus purely on survival the management may start to plan for growth. The aims and objectives may change in response to developments internally, such as the performance of the business and other internal reasons. Or there may be external factors such as changes in market conditions, technology or legislation.

Why? (Grade 6)

A business may start for personal reasons, such as to be your own boss. But once the business is up and running, the owner may want more – perhaps to develop a shop into a business empire, as happened with a coffee shop on Waterloo station called Costa. So objectives and ambitions change over time. They may also change because of circumstances, such as a sudden, exciting opportunity because of new legislation.

How? (Grade 7)

To set about changing your aims and objectives it's vital to talk long and hard with your key managers and staff. If they dislike your plans, they may need a rethink. If you're still sure, focus on how to achieve the objectives – and make sure every staff member knows their role.

So? (Grade 8)

The world is always changing, so it's important to rethink your objectives when market conditions or technology moves on. If an American tax cut opens up opportunities for UK exports, a new sales target may be called for. That should help motivate staff to take advantage of this situation, providing a big opportunity to boost revenue and profits.

Grade 9

However, there can be risks when aims and objectives change. Toyota spent 50 years building a reputation for the world's most reliable cars. Then the aim changed: to become the world's Number 1 carmaker. Quality took a backseat as the business launched new car models to make more sales. Suddenly, in 2010, a story broke about safety problems in Toyotas sold in America and China. The problems cost $billions to solve before the grandson of the original 'Mr Toyota' took back control and re-set quality and reliability as the key aims.

> **Do** think about factors relating to change, such as deciding whether to enter new markets, or exit existing ones. Rolls Royce once made marine (ship) engines, but decided to exit the market in 2018

> **Don't** ignore the effects of decisions such as exiting a market: this might mean reducing the workforce – with important effects on the people and families involved.

> **Exam tip**: remember that aims state where you want to go and objectives give clear signs of what you want to achieve and by when, e.g. increase market share to 22% by 2022.

Changes in Aims: 5-step logic chain (to get to the top level of response)

Chain 1. Sensible entrepreneurs start up with the aim of survival – to get through the super-tough first year (1) … but then may change to an aim such as to boost profit to over £50,000 a year (2). But even if the business has been going well, a sudden decline in market conditions might force a re-set back to survival (3) … perhaps by focusing on cash flow factors such as getting customers to pay promptly (4) to get through the tough period and then, later, re-focus on new, more positive, aims. (5)

Chain 2. If aims are switched from sales growth to profit growth (1) … it may be sensible to cut back on the product range. (2) If too many product lines are made it may be hard to keep control of costs and stock (3) … so cutting out the smaller-selling, less profitable lines can cut total costs (4) … making it easier to turn sales revenue into net profit. (5)

Stakeholders

What? (Grade 5 basics)

Stakeholders are the groups that have an interest in the success or failure of a business. Internal stakeholders serve the organisation. They include employees, managers and shareholders. External stakeholders are affected by the organisation, such as suppliers, the local community, pressure groups, customers and the government.

Why? (Grade 6)

Businesses are at the heart of our economy and society. The decisions they make can generate high-paying jobs and wealth, or can treat customers or staff with contempt. Encouraging business leaders to think of all their stakeholders may help bring about decisions that are fairer to weak and strong alike.

How? (Grade 7)

Business decisions must always reflect the profit to be made. But business leaders could take greater account of what is fair to stakeholders. Partly because that's morally right, but also in the best long-term interests of the business. Staff that are fairly treated are more likely to stay – and more likely to work hard to help the business prosper.

So? (Grade 8)

Big businesses with a focus on long-term success will think about the best interests of stakeholders – and may even bring the stakeholders into the planning process. Internal stakeholders are especially likely to have valuable thoughts about making the business better and more successful. Who understands a school better than the teachers and the students? Talking to key stakeholders can be a huge step forward.

Grade 9

But it's wrong to think that all business leaders think this way. Many feel too much pressure on their shoulders to think what's best for the long-term future. They are trying to cope with today. So they concentrate on what the shareholders want. And what they usually want is a clear sign that profits are rising. This makes it vital to show that profit <u>now</u> is higher than profit 6 or 12 months' ago. So instead of thinking about all the stakeholders, decisions end up being made for short-term profit.

> **Do** consider the importance of external stakeholders in a social media world. A Twitter-storm of hostility to a business might come from unhappy customers or local residents. And that's bad news.

> **Don't** try to cover all the stakeholders when answering a 9 or 12-mark question. Pick two stakeholders that are important to the specific business

> **Exam tip:** many answers can be based on stakeholders v shareholders. In some cases leaders focus only on shareholders (and therefore profit) while others think about all the stakeholders

---

Stakeholders: 5-step logic chain (to get to the top level of response)

Chain 1. When businesses start up, they have to focus on cash flow and profit (1) … because if the business doesn't survive, no-one can benefit from it (2). But once the business is established and profitable decisions can take stakeholders into account (3) … such as checking on whether suppliers are looking after their staff properly (4) or giving your own staff a more enjoyable, social workplace – perhaps including buying the first round of drinks for all staff every Friday night. (5)

Chain 2. Private limited companies can grow to become quite large (1) … with family shareholders who may care a lot about the annual profit being made. (2) The business leader may feel pressured to make decisions based on the highest profits possible (3) … but that may weaken long-term customer or employee loyalty (4) … undermining the long-term growth prospects of the business. (5)

Stakeholder effects

What? (Grade 5 basics)

Businesses affect stakeholders in every decision they take – good or bad. Marks & Spencer closing 100 shops means thousands of job losses – but perhaps a higher company-wide profit for shareholders. And stakeholders can affect businesses, e.g. when high street banks forced small companies to close during the 2009 recession.

Stakeholders ⟷ Companies

Why? (Grade 6)

Stakeholders are at the heart of companies' activities, successes and failures. There's no such a thing as a company without directors and employees (internal) or suppliers and customers (external). So it's inevitable that stakeholder actions affect companies – and company actions affect stakeholders.

How? (Grade 7)

Companies have to respond to changes in external conditions, e.g. the shift to online sales. This may involve changing staff requirements – fewer sales staff, but more IT staff. Unless staff can re-train (which would be hard), there will be redundancies followed by the recruitment of new people. This means a sharp effect on staff as stakeholders.

So? (Grade 8)

Senior management should try always to balance the needs of different stakeholders and find a reasonable course between their different interests. If every decision seems to be in favour of shareholders, staff and customers may feel the company isn't for them. In tough times staff will understand that cutbacks may be necessary for the business to survive. But when times are good it's important that the company should share its wealth with staff and management – instead of simply making directors and shareholders richer.

Grade 9

The effect of stakeholders on business is seen most clearly in pressure from shareholders (to boost profit), from bankers (to repay loans) and from customers (to respond to changing tastes, e.g. towards 'free-from'. Senior managers may be able to hold off the views of the shareholders or bankers, but cannot ignore the customers. Even if a bakery believes gluten-free bread is inferior to ordinary bread, 'the customer is always right'. Arrogant managers don't last long.

Do consider whether it's possible to keep every stakeholder happy. The owner of *The Entertainer* toy shops keeps the stores closed on Sundays for the benefit of staff. Many young customers may be less happy.

Don't make it sound as if every business has a sole focus on profits and shareholders. Many have, it's true, but others have a genuine desire to care for staff & customers.

Exam tip: student answers can be a bit timid. Be prepared to criticise a business that seems to ignore the needs of a key stakeholder group. For example discrimination by race or gender is bad business as well as unethical.

Stakeholder effects: 5-step logic chain (to get to the top level of response)

Chain 1. The effect of a business on its stakeholders can be dreadful (1) … such as poor safety standards on an airplane or a fast-food business persuading children to eat unhealthily (2). Shareholders should care what's done in their name, but may focus too much on short-term profit (3) … making it necessary, sometimes, for government to step in (4) … perhaps by initiating new laws to control business behaviour. (5)

Chain 2. Stakeholders' actions can damage the business they have an interest in (1) … such as a supplier making an unsuccessful move to change its production method (2) … causing erratic deliveries of a key production component (3) … and therefore bringing production to a halt (4). This might lead customers to look elsewhere, making it near-impossible to overcome the damage caused. (5)

Organic growth

What? (Grade 5 basics)

A business can achieve growth from within (organic growth) or by external means such as buying up a rival company. Internal growth can come from developing new products or finding new customers in new markets. In both cases the planning and the effort comes from within the business, e.g. clever marketing staff finding a new type of customer.

Why? (Grade 6)

Organic (internal) growth is beneficial because your own staff are the ones developing the new opportunities. This is better than writing out a cheque to buy up a rival, because staff build careers based on their own success. Google has bought some other businesses, but most of its growth has come organically – which is why staff are so proud to work there.

How? (Grade 7)

To grow organically you need to understand your customers well enough to see what extra services they may require – and how their tastes may develop in future (think iPhone after iPhone). This may require big spending on consumer market research plus Research & Development to try to find innovative new products. A business that grows externally may be trying to cover up its own failings by buying up better rival businesses.

So? (Grade 8)

News programmes love a take-over because it means something exciting happening in the business world. But staff don't find it exciting to have their jobs threatened – and customers may hate to lose 'their' Cadbury or McVities to a foreign owner. So organic growth is much more likely to benefit the stakeholders in a business – and is also more likely to help the country's economic growth rate. External growth is over-rated.

Grade 9

The best thing about organic growth is that it tends to be slow and steady. It's like a twiggy young tree growing over the years into something substantial, with a strong trunk and a big canopy of green leaves and shoots. Buying up another business means a sudden leap forward in the company's size and scale – and many managers find that this is very hard to handle. A five-year-old may yearn to become an adult overnight – but it's hard to see it working out well.

> **Do** think about new markets as well as new products. It's still called organic growth even if it's a UK company opening its first outlets in China or Vietnam

> **Don't** make growth sound too easy. Cash flow comes under serious pressure when businesses grow rapidly – such as when two companies merge

> **Exam tip**: remember that organic growth can come from increasing output, gaining new customers, developing new products or by increasing your market share.

Organic growth: 5-step logic chain (to get to the top level of response)

Chain 1. Growing successfully by takeover requires a huge amount of management skill (1) ... perhaps more skill than most managers actually have (2). Growing organically is better because it's a bit slower and therefore more controllable (3) ... and because it's built on the career success of your own staff (4) ... just like a football team built on local talent, not bought-in from the outside. (5)

Chain 2. To grow organically, a business needs new ideas for products/services backed by new technology (1) ... therefore making it hard for competitors to keep up (2) ... allowing your organic growth to come from your increasing market share (3). Growing by looking overseas is risky (4) ... for every success (Costa; Burberry) there are overseas flops (M&S; Tesco). (5)

Business Growth: external

What? (Grade 5 basics)

There are two ways of growing by changing the ownership structure. One is to combine permanently with a business of similar size; this is called a merger. The other is for a big business to take over a smaller one – perhaps adding 25% to the size of the business - instantly.

Why? (Grade 6)

Business bosses are often impatient. They want to achieve something big – perhaps becoming the No 1 in their market – and want to achieve it NOW! So instead of steadily working away at building market share, they make a take-over bid for a rival. If they succeed they may become Number 1 overnight. So external growth by takeover or merger can be very attractive.

And bosses love to be in control. So they like a horizontal takeover that gives control over a rival, but also vertical control over a supplier or a customer. In the case of the third category – diversification – the business gains greater control over uncertainty.

How? (Grade 7)

To take over another company you make a bid by offering a higher price per share than their current stock market value. So if the market price of your rivals' shares is £7, you might bid £9. If most of the rival's shareholders sell to you, you can achieve full control. To merge, you just need the agreement of the main directors and shareholders.

So? (Grade 8)

Takeovers can work out brilliantly for the companies, such as Google buying Youtube or Mars buying Wrigley's. In both cases they extended the company's reach into their market – and boosted profits. But Google itself has had several disasters, including buying Motorola for $12billion – then selling it for $3billion just two years' later. Even for a giant such as Google, a $9 billion loss hurts.

So takeovers should be undertaken with huge care. The same goes for mergers, which can also turn out badly.

Grade 9

No-one can be sure whether a takeover or merger will work out well or badly. But one thing is certain. If the takeover is financed by debt, the risks of failure become hugely greater. In January 2018 the huge Carillion construction group collapsed. It was weighed down by debts after going on a takeover spending spree.

> **Do** show the examiner you understand the risks involved in buying a business you don't know and understand. The 2010 take-over of Blackburn Rovers FC by an egg producer from India proved a disaster.

> **Don't** forget the possible impact of a takeover on the customers. They rarely gain.

> **Exam tip**: the exam board loves balanced answers and here's a great topic. Takeovers have positives but also many possible negatives. Good to remember for the conclusion that research shows that about two thirds of mergers & takeovers prove a disappointment

---

Business Growth: 5-step logic chain (getting to the top response level)

Chain 1. A merger may seem a clever way out of a problem, e.g. when there are two struggling companies (1) ... but putting two messes together tends to make a bigger mess (2) ... because a bigger business is harder to manage (3). The biggest problems tend to be to do with staff morale and focus (4) ... so a positive sign is when the boss-to-be has a strong record at managing people. (5)

Chain 2. When a small business buys another the problems are especially bad (1) ... because small firms are dominated by one individual – who usually feels like the expert (2) ... so every idea from the outside is inevitably 'bad'(3) ... leading to arguments and disputes (4)... which can rub off onto staff or customers – making the new combined business less pleasant to do business with. (5)

Answering exams

OCR produces sample exam papers to help teachers. In these there is one question directly about takeovers. But in OCR's marking guidance there are plenty of mentions of takeovers. It is a topic that helps in answering many different questions about business strategy.

Here are 3 questions where changes in ownership are a significant part of the answer:

P2 Q7a) Define the term 'takeover'. (1 mark)

P2 Q7e) Evaluate whether Sainsbury's is likely to benefit from its takeover of Home Retail Group. You should use the information provided as well as your knowledge of business. (12 marks)

Q3. Discuss whether a fast-growing, family-owned online retailer should become a plc to help finance growth. (6)

On the right are strong answers to these three questions. They are models for writing about takeovers rather than models for how to score 6 or 12 marks.

Grade 9 Answers (see questions on the left)

7a) A takeover occurs when one company buys a majority of the shares in another company, thereby taking full control.

7e) Sainsbury's took over Home Retail Group ('Argos') in order to strengthen its market position and profit. Figure 4 shows that Argos has almost as many stores as Sainsburys, but they make about a tenth of the profit. So putting some Argos stores into Sainsburys – to cut down on the number on the high street – seems a good one. It should cut out a lot of the fixed costs the business used to face.

However, if Sainsbury was struggling with Lidl/Aldi while Argos was battling Amazon, perhaps the two businesses are too weak to get together. Perhaps they would each have been better off fighting their individual battles rather than trying to fight side-by-side. Two weak businesses rarely combine into one strong one.

On balance Sainsbury seems unlikely to benefit from this takeover. Research shows that most takeovers prove disappointing. It is hard to see why this should be any different.

Q3. Becoming a plc means that shares can be advertised to outsiders, perhaps by floating the company onto the stock market. This can bring lots of extra share capital – all at once. If growth is rapid, there's probably a need for a lot of extra finance – so this method would work.

However, selling shares to outsiders may mean losing the family's control of 50+% of the share capital. Down the line, others may be able to build a majority shareholding and get rid of the founder and other family directors.

The Purpose of Marketing

What? (Grade 5 basics)

Marketing is the department that identifies the customers that should be targeted, finds out their wants and needs, then works out how best to communicate a message that will persuade them to buy. In this way, marketing tries to establish a profitable sales level for a business, then find ways to increase sales.

Why? (Grade 6)

However good your product or service, modern markets are so crowded that it's easy to disappear. It would be nice to be so successful that word-of-mouth and social media keep customers coming. But for most businesses it's vital to keep telling customers about your qualities and strengths. That keeps existing customers coming back for more, and encourages new ones to try you out.

> **Do** remember that marketing is the business's way of influencing its revenue. The better the marketing, the higher the revenue

How? (Grade 7)

Marketing begins with market research, in other words finding out as much as possible about the buying habits and attitudes of potential customers. From that, managers can work out who to target (15-22-year-old women, perhaps), what message to use and how best to get that message across: cinema advertising, maybe? Or Snapchat?

> **Don't** confuse marketing with advertising. Marketing involves many different things such as pricing. It's not just advertising.

So? (Grade 8)

Marketing is a vital influence on one of the key numbers in business: revenue. Marketing has an effect on both the components of revenue: the price you charge and the volume of sales you make. So even if marketing spending is quite expensive it may be vital for the financial health of the business.

Grade 9

Marketing is changing rapidly as businesses try to keep up with how customers live today. No more whole families watching TV commercials in X Factor. As it gets harder – and more expensive – to persuade new customers to try new products, marketing focuses more on keeping existing customers loyal. It's cheaper to keep a customer than to find a new one. That's why coffee bars have those Buy 5 get One Free cards and clever businesses focus hugely on customer service.

> **Exam tip:** even though marketing can boost revenue, it is expensive to do well. Therefore spending more on marketing may add more to costs than to revenue. That would cut profit rather than boost it.

Customer needs: 5-step logic chain (necessary to get to the top response level)

Chain 1. To increase sales a business may decide to spend more on marketing (1) … which might begin with extra spending on market research (2) … to get new insights into what consumers want today. (3) From this it may become clear the business needs a new approach to advertising (4) … perhaps switching spending to social media to attract younger buyers (5)

Chain 2. When a new product is being launched the starting point may be to inform customers (1) … so that they know the new product exists, i.e. have product awareness (2). From this starting point the key will be to persuade people to buy their first one, i.e. product trial (3) … and then work hard to turn that trial into repeat purchase (4) helped, perhaps, by building a strong, attractive brand. (5)

Understanding Customers

What? (Grade 5 basics)

Customer needs include the right product of the right quality at an affordable price. Customers also need a wide range of choice (to suit their needs) and are willing to pay for convenience.

Why? (Grade 6)

It is important to identify and understand customer needs in order to generate sales and to help the business survive in a competitive world. If a business fails to understand the needs of its customers it is leaving itself exposed to attack from current or new competitors. If you're offering white sliced while your customers want organic wholemeal, you're in trouble.

How? (Grade 7)

To identify your customers it's hard to beat online registration. In a few moments you can find out your customers' age, address and gender. To understand them is harder, but can be done through qualitative market research. Many large companies run monthly surveys to measure any shifts in customer attitudes. This might show that customers no longer need to find low-fat foods, because their focus has shifted to low-carb.

So? (Grade 8)

It isn't easy to turn a business idea into big profits. To achieve success, nothing is more important than understanding your customers – and then focusing the business on meeting their needs. So it's important to monitor social media to keep listening to what's being thought and said about you.

Grade 9

At the highest level, unpick whether the issue is really customer *needs*. Isn't it really customer *wants*? In countries like Britain many people spend much of their income on wants rather than needs. I may tell myself 'I need a Snickers' but really I mean 'I want a Snickers'. Companies can be quite cunning at persuading us to buy more of what we don't need. So whereas companies might talk about their ability to meet customer needs, they often mean wants.

> **Do** consider that different people may have different needs – which may make it sensible to segment the market and offer different products

> **Don't** forget that customer needs are changing constantly, forcing companies to adapt existing products or launch new ones.

> **Exam tip:** customer needs are affected by their psychology, so qualitative research tends to be especially important.

Customer needs: 5-step logic chain (necessary to get to the top response level)

Chain 1. Customer needs can change with different fashions and trends (1) ... so businesses need to know what's happening on the street (2) ... then be bold about changing in line with trends (3) before new or existing rivals get there first (4) The more fashion-focused the market sector the more important this is. (5)

Chain 2. Companies sometimes hide behind the term customer needs, when they really mean 'wants' (1) ... In other words persuading customers to think they 'need' a new phone or a box of Lindor when they really just *want* one. (2) This means manipulating customers rather than serving them (3) ... possibly into buying things that are bad/fattening for them (4) which may be good business but is definitely questionable ethically. (5)

Market research - Purpose

What? (Grade 5 basics)

There are four main reasons why businesses spend their money and time on market research: to identify and understand customer needs; to identify gaps in the market; to provide the information needed to take business decisions and therefore reduce the risks involved.

Why? (Grade 6)

A shop owner running a bakery may deal with customers daily and know their likes and dislikes. A boss running a bigger, nation-wide business cannot meet all the customers, so market research is a way to keep in touch. The boss can read regular reports on customer comments, praise and complaints. And when big decisions have to be made, market research provides the information to help do the right thing.

How? (Grade 7)

Methods of carrying out market research can be grouped into primary and secondary. They are explained in the following chapter.

So? (Grade 8)

In business, you should never think in isolation. If company A is thinking about launching a new product or switching to e-commerce/online sales only, company B is probably thinking the same way. Market research is needed to give company A the edge: to help make a slightly better decision. The Sony PS4 wasn't that much better than the Xbox One – yet it's outsold XBox 2:1 globally.

Grade 9

The purpose of market research is to make better marketing decisions and therefore reduce the risk of failure. But fewer than 1 in 5 new products succeeds in the UK. Two years' after launch, 4 out of 5 have disappeared. Many will have used market research to help reduce the level of risk, but nothing can reduce that risk level to zero. Intelligent businesspeople use market research as an aid to decision-making, acting boldly where necessary, e.g. scrapping a new product before launch because the research findings are good – but not good enough.

> **Do** ask whether the business decision is important enough to justify spending £000s on market research. It's not always.

> **Don't** forget to match the purpose of the research to the method, e.g. if the purpose is background information, secondary research may be ideal.

> **Exam tip:** show the examiner you understand that small businesses often know their customers so well that there's no need to spend money on market research.

Market research purpose: 5-step logic chain (getting to the top response level)

Chain 1. If a company's sales are slipping it needs to find out why (1) ... so businesses need to find out what customers are thinking and where they're going (2) ... and the sooner the business can find out the quicker it can react (3) ... ideally before its competitors (4) When the business is clear on the purpose of the research it can think about the type of research needed, i.e. the research method. (5)

Chain 2. Market research is expensive and therefore needs to have a clear purpose (1) ... such as identifying whether a big enough gap exists in the market to enable a new product to be launched successfully. (2) This means finding out what consumers *really* want from this type of product (3) ... and where competitors are failing to provide what customers need or want. (4) If market research can unpick this information and helps launch a new product success, it'll be worth every penny. (5)

Section 2.2: Market Research

Market research: methods and use of data

What? (Grade 5 basics)

Market research methods can be grouped into two categories: primary and secondary. Primary research is carried out first-hand, asking selected people their views on topics a company wants answered directly, e.g. would you buy our new Orange Maltesers? Secondary research is second-hand, such as finding out from government statistics that the number of 15-19-year-olds in the UK is forecast to rise by 450,000 between 2020 and 2025. The data collected by research can be quantitative (statistical) or qualitative (psychological).

Why? (Grade 6)

The different types of research do different jobs. If Ford decided to launch an electric-powered bike, it would need to find out general (secondary) information about the market for bikes e.g. what's the market size? What's the market growth? Then it might decide to discover more about the psychology of owning and choosing a bike; therefore it would use primary research in a qualitative way, perhaps using focus groups of 6 – 8 bike owners. Later on it might conduct a primary survey to get quantitative data to help forecast the likely level of sales for an electric bike (in Japan more than 500,000 'e-bikes' are sold each year, at over £500 each).

How? (Grade 7)

Secondary research is done at your desk, probably starting with Google. Primary research must be done specifically, probably using an independent research company. Quantitative surveys can easily cost £10,000 and even small-scale qualitative research can cost £5,000+. A further issue here is how long? Primary research can take several weeks from start to final results – and some businesses worry about delays – especially when they're about to launch a new product.

So? (Grade 8)

Big decisions can make or lose a lot of money, so the choice of market research method is important. Some big businesses use research for every element of every decision. That's expensive and time-consuming, but can help prevent business disasters such as Samsung's launch of its Note 7 (the exploding one) or Cadbury's £4 million launch of 'Puddles' in 2015 – that's OK, no-one else remembers it. For Puddles, Cadbury used qualitative research that pointed towards young people as the target market. They weren't. Choosing the right method is vital.

Grade 9

Market research has to be reliable. That can only be achieved if the sample of people questioned is unbiased, i.e. truly represents people within the target market. For quantitative research there's another requirement – that the sample size should be big enough to give reliable data (perhaps 500-1,000 people). With reliability can come accuracy. And that enables marketing managers to draw clear conclusions – such as that the planned new product has a strong chance of succeeding. In the case of Cadbury and Puddles, that didn't happen.

Do consider whether the business needs psychological insights or numbers, e.g. to make a sales forecast.

Don't over-estimate the value of market research. Apple used no market research before launching its hugely successful iPad or iPhone. It believed it understood its customers well enough to know what they wanted.

Exam tip: be firm in your conclusions about any data presented by the examiner. Too many students dither; top students are decisive – and give clear, firm reasoning for their decision.

Market research methods: 5-step logic chain (necessary for top response level)

Chain 1. For a new business start-up it's best to start with secondary research (1) … as lots is free and is available at public libraries and by Googling. (2) Having gained a broad understanding of the market an entrepreneur can focus on a specific market segment (3) … perhaps using primary research in the form of a qualitative focus group (4) … then use the insights gained to draw up a questionnaire to be used for quantitative research, then a sales forecast (5)

Chain 2. A famous business phrase is 'paralysis by analysis' (1) … which can happen when a business gathers so much market research information that managers struggle to reach a conclusion (2). This may lead to decisions being postponed because arrows pointing in one direction seem countered by others pointing elsewhere. (3) Market research should help in making decisions, not bog them down (4) … but this will only happen if the managers have clear objectives and the ability to be decisive. (5)

Answering exams

OCR regularly tests market research with direct questions. It is important to remember, though, that many other questions in business point to the need for research. A good example is shown below, in answer to Q2. Every Paper 1 exam contains one 7 and one 9-mark question asking you to evaluate a business problem. Market research will often be an important part of a good answer.

Q1. Analyse one way in which McDonald's could use quantitative research. (3)

Q2. At their bakery, Neil and Sue are considering two options to reduce the amount they need to sell to break even.

Option 1: Increasing average prices by 10%

Option 2: Reducing the cost of ingredients by using a cheaper supplier

Justify which one of these two options Neil and Sue should choose. (9 marks)

On the right are strong answers to these two questions. The answer to Q2 shows how to use market research effectively.

Grade 9 Answers (questions on left)

Q1. One way would be to interview people who have not been to McDonalds for the past 6 months. They could be asked questions about why they haven't been, where they go instead and what might attract them to McDonalds in future. If the sample size is large enough it could help the business make decisions about new menu items to attract new (or returning) customers.

Q2. A 10% price increase is a serious possibility. Neil and Sue's bakery and café 'has a lot of passing trade' and their traditional baking methods and high-quality ingredients are likely to give them a high degree of product (service) differentiation. Furthermore the text makes no mention of competition. With a revamp of the technology to reduce the queueing time, it's very possible that the bakery will end up with the same number of customers, but at 10% more revenue per sale.

By contrast, 'using a cheaper supplier' may put the whole business at risk. OK, it's conceivable that they've found someone to supply the same high-quality ingredients at a lower price, but surely it's more likely that the lower prices are due to lower standards. Customers used to quality can be unforgiving if standards slip.

If Neil and Sue are in doubt about what to do, the obvious solution is quantitative market research among existing customers. At the moment that will be easy to do: interview people as they queue. It seems overwhelmingly likely that the bakery's regulars will opt for higher prices than a risk of slipping standards.

Use and Interpretation of market research

What? (Grade 5 basics)

Qualitative data is used to make judgements, such as: 'Do customers really love Jamie's Italian, or do they just love Jamie Oliver?' This relies on accurate interpretation of the comments customers make during in-depth interviews. By contrast quantitative data provides numbers that need little interpretation, e.g. 69% of 15-19-year-olds don't like being seen in Marks & Spencer.

Why? (Grade 6)

Especially in a world of Facebook Likes and online surveys it's easy for businesses to collect huge amounts of market research data. A second-rate manager would select the data that supports his/her argument, then use it to prove to a boss that his/her work is great. That Debenhams is doing fine, or that the shift to vegan diets is temporary. So it's vital to treat market research data seriously, and make sure to avoid any bias in its use or interpretation.

How? (Grade 7)

To avoid bias, the key is to ask the data questions, rather than search for answers. Somewhere out there is a student who likes my teaching! So my temptation is to sift through until I find it. Better is to ask a question such as: What is the age profile of our Facebook Likes compared with Dislikes? If the Likes have an average age of 22 and the Dislikes 34, it might be fair to think things are going well.

So? (Grade 8)

The greatest use of market research would be to see where customer thoughts or behaviours are heading. All decisions are about the future, so a hint about next month or next year would be marvellous. Someone in a group discussion may have swapped their car for an electric bike – and others may be really envious. Perhaps a new trend is on its way.

Grade 9

In exams you'll have to interpret research results that may be shown as a bar or pie chart. You must calmly use the figures and look for patterns (perhaps change since last year). This takes a lot of practice, but is a skill expected of a top student.

> **Do** ask whether an important decision should ever be based on the views of a handful of people – as is true of qualitative research.

> **Don't** hesitate to question whether bias has crept into the research, e.g. in the way it's being interpreted. Ambitious managers often exaggerate the strength of customer opinion.

> **Exam tip:** read the question two or three times if it mentions qualitative or quantitative research. You mustn't muddle them up!

Use of market research: 5-step logic chain (getting to the top response level)

Chain 1. It's important in business to spot trends early (1) ... so regular research among existing customers is great, to get the first hint of them being fed up with you (2) ... and therefore being able to address the problem before it becomes a disaster (3) If customers say your service is getting worse (4) ... you want the problem tackled before it starts to hill weekly sales. (5)

Chain 2. Market research is expensive but nothing like as costly as making a big marketing mistake (1) ... such as launching a new product that flops. (2) Effective interpretation of research requires a lot of experience and therefore reliable, long-standing staff (3) ... so a well-run human resources department can be as important as marketing (4)... in helping to keep and motivate your best research staff (5)

Market Segmentation

What? (Grade 5 basics)

Segmentation means identifying the different customer groups within your market. A market can be segmented by age (young to old), by income (rich to poor), by lifestyle (trendy to traditional), by gender (male/female) or by location/geography (town to country or north to south).

Why? (Grade 6)

When a brand new product is launched, it may be designed to appeal to as many people as possible. But it probably can't be perfect for everyone. So, in the UK market for smartphones, there are phones designed for older customers (bigger buttons, fewer functions and simpler to operate). Segmentation can help expand the market size – some older people wouldn't bother with an ordinary smartphone but are happy to buy a simpler model.

How? (Grade 7)

Use research to see whether different market segments would prefer different products. Currently Ferrero's chocolate market share is booming in China and India thanks to their success targeting young children with Kinder Eggs.

So? (Grade 8)

It's very hard for new businesses to compete head-on with established giants such as Heinz or Cadbury. So it's cleverer to identify a small-ish segment that could be better served with a well-designed product. This enables the new business to establish itself – and gives a group of customers just what they want.

Grade 9

When a market is growing (think smartphones in 2014-2018) it's quite easy to find new ways to segment it. New opportunities open up. But it's much harder to segment a long-established market such as baked beans or bread; all the easy segmentation gaps have been filled. So lifestyle changes can be very important. In recent years, with the bread market in decline, '*Genius*' gluten-free bread has grown from nothing to £30 million of sales a year. Genius.

Do realise that segmentation has a downside: the smaller the target segment, the harder for sales revenues to cover all the costs of development, launch and production

Don't ignore lifestyle as a source of segmentation. It changes as fashions change, so it always throws up new business opportunities

Exam tip: use market segmentation as the starting point to analyse how firms try to avoid competing head-on with rivals. It's easier to make a profit if you're the only brand in a market segment.

Market segmentation: 5-step logic chain (getting to the top response level)

Chain 1. Segmentation is a good way for a new business to find a market gap (1) … perhaps identifying that current shampoos aren't suited to older people's hair (2) so using demographic segmentation to identify a gap (3) … then design a product to meet the needs of customers in this segment (4) … allowing the product – at launch – to be priced a little higher than other shampoos. (5)

Chain 2. Because product life cycles come to an end, big companies need to keep launching new products; as the centre of the market may be crowded, segmentation may help (1) … perhaps in spotting that breakfast habits are different in cities than elsewhere. (2) This enabled Mondelez to spot the opportunity for its Belvita breakfast biscuit (3) … that families with an over-stretched lifestyle use as breakfast-on-the-go (4) …. allowing a chocolate and biscuit-maker to break into the breakfast market that used to be dominated by Kelloggs. (5)

Introduction to the Marketing Mix

What? (Grade 5 basics)

The marketing mix is the way a business uses 4 factors to turn its marketing ideas into a clear plan. The four are product, price, promotion and place; so the marketing mix is often called the '4Ps'. A successful mix is one that achieves the marketing objectives of the business, such as to build market share or to outsell a rival.

Why? (Grade 6)

The importance of the mix is that the 4 factors have to be coordinated with care. In other words it's no good having glossy advertisements in Vogue and the Sunday Times if you're going to promote your product by shouting Buy One Get One Free! The image and the reality will clash (what if Mercedes promoted its cars with Buy One Get One Free??).

How? (Grade 7)

The starting point is to decide where to target your product (at a niche market perhaps?). Then:

- design the right Product to meet the needs and wants of that type of customer
- set the Price that matches those customers' expectations and incomes
- Promote the product in the right way (social media for a younger niche; TV for an older target market)
- then find the best way to Place your product in the right distribution channels to make it easy for customers to purchase

So? (Grade 8)

Getting the mix right is partly down to a good marketing team and partly down to the competitive environment. For many years Next plc seemed to be doing brilliantly in the clothing market; with hindsight its success was a lot to do with the failings of its main rival: Marks & Spencer. Your business might want to set high prices for its product, but if a close rival is setting lower prices, you may have to keep prices down. Decisions on the marketing mix need to bear in mind the competitive environment.

Grade 9

Getting the right, balanced marketing mix is hard. Even harder is successfully keeping up with changes in the marketplace. The competitive environment may be transformed by an Uber-type of new competitor. Or customer needs may change, as in 2018 when the demand for diesel cars fell sharply, with a clear switch to electric. No less important has been the impact of technology, with some traditional businesses being slow to switch to digital communication (advertising through social media) and to e-commerce.

Do focus on the need for the 4Ps to fit together and work together. And be willing to speak out if a business has one 'P' out of line from the other three.

Don't make this part of business seem easy. Businesses as big as Mars and Toyota have struggled to find the right mix in the new high-tech, online era.

Exam tip: examiners love it when students are bold. If you criticise a company's low prices while all other students are praising them – your answer stands out – and makes your answer more interesting for the examiner

The marketing mix: 5-step logic chain (to get to the top response level)

Chain 1. A successful marketing mix needs the 4Ps to work well together (1) … based on understanding and meeting customer needs (2) … so that the price charged seems right for the product on offer (3) … and the methods of promotion reach the right people in a way that takes them from product awareness to product purchase (4) … with the distribution methods making it easy for people to buy what they want when they want. (5)

Chain 2. A service business needs a different mix from a producer (1) … often based on providing a more individualised 'product' (2) .., such as Starbucks with its amazing range of choice (3). Other mix factors matter, such as promoting the brand name and the idea of service and variety (4) backed by store locations placed for customer convenience and a price people are willing to pay (5).

Answering exams

OCR produces sample exam papers to help teachers. In these there are several questions about the marketing mix. There are also broader questions in which a paragraph on the '4Ps' would be very useful. Here are two questions:

Q1. Analyse one method of promotion that would be appropriate for *ASOS*. (3 marks)

Q2. Neil and Sue are considering two options to reduce the amount they need to sell to break even at their bakery.

Option 1: Increasing average prices by 10%

Option 2: Reducing the cost of ingredients by using a cheaper supplier.

Justify which one of these two options Neil and Sue should choose. (9 marks)

For more on exam technique see Section 3.

Grade 9 Answers (Qs. on the left)

Q1. The most appropriate for ASOS is to spend heavily online, largely through social media. If the brand keeps circulating positive messages about its quality of design and speed of service, young adults will continue to see it as preferable to an older brand such as Marks and Spencer.

Q2. Option 1 suggests a 10% price rise. But this has been put forward in isolation – ignoring the other aspects of the marketing mix. Although Meringue's 'place' is ideal – with lots of passing trade – a glance at the photo shows a pretty basic sandwich bar: not a shop that can easily support sharp price rises. While at this location it would be hard to justify a price rise.

And then there's Option 2, which threatens to reduce the quality reputation for product by focusing on getting a cheaper supplier. This, in turn, could threaten the long-term position of the business. If products are 'high quality' one minute, it's risky to undercut that by buying more cheaply unless you're certain that the actual quality of the ingredients in unchanged.

Further Exam tip. Several OCR questions adopt a similar pattern of 'Analyse one way …' and then give two or three options that must be looked at. Frequently this question will be based on choosing two or more elements of the mix.

Product

What? (Grade 5 basics)

A successful product or service needs to be designed to meet customer needs and wants. This usually requires a careful balance between three things: function (how it works), appeal to the senses and the cost of production. If the target market is cash-poor students, the design must be simple enough to allow low-cost production and therefore low prices. If the product is well enough designed it should have a long product life cycle – thanks to customers staying loyal for many, many years.

Why? (Grade 6)

Products must be well designed because they are at the heart of the marketing mix. Pricing, place and promotion cannot help if the product is dreadful. So companies can take years to develop the product with the right design mix. The design of the first Tesla electric car focused on looks and function, with little regard for economic manufacture. Therefore it was expensive to make, and carried a high price tag, but quickly became the world's best-selling plug-in electric car. In many market sectors, customers are prepared to pay for quality.

How? (Grade 7)

The best designs start with a great understanding of how consumers behave and think – so market research is a good starting point. Good designers can turn customers' thoughts and needs into a design that stands out from the crowd. But design is more than the look and feel – it must also cover function – how well the product achieves its purpose. Does the robotic vacuum-cleaner really clean well? And is it quiet enough to avoid scaring pets?

So? (Grade 8)

If the design balance is right, customers will happily pay prices that yield high profits. And that allows the product to have a long life cycle, backed by consistent advertising spending and money spent in maintaining high distribution levels. Eventually sales will flatten out (reach maturity), making it time to start designing a new product to be launched when the older one is in decline.

Grade 9

You will know that the ideal marketing mix is based on linking the '4Ps' cleverly. And that the 4Ps together must match the customer need or market gap. But generally it is wrong to think of the 4Ps as being of equal value. The most important is Product. If the right product (or service) has been designed correctly to meet the precise needs of the market segment – it will take some stopping. The other 3Ps must be built around the Product. If a stylish Product is aimed at 20-30-year-olds with high spending power, the Price can be high, the Promotion focused on social media plus high-impact cinema advertising and the Place being trendy shops plus online.

Do think about the horizontal axis on a product life cycle diagram, i.e. Time. Cadbury's Dairy Milk was launched in 1905 – and is still in its maturity phase. Some products last centuries, others last only weeks, eg Loom Bands

Don't forget that invention is having a new idea; innovation is bringing that new idea to the marketplace

Exam tip: it's helpful to see Product at the heart of the marketing mix. Once that's been decided on the other three elements of the mix are much easier to handle.

> **Product: 5-step logic chain (necessary to get to the top response level)**
>
> **Chain 1.** A well-designed Product is at the heart of a successful marketing mix (1) … especially if good design turns an invention into a well-thought-out innovation (2). Good design adds value to a product, partly through distinctiveness (3) … which, in turn, helps to keep customers loyal (4) … and forms the basis for building a powerful brand name. (5)
>
> **Chain 2.** A short product life cycle may be measured only in months (1) … forcing the business to work constantly on new products to replace older ones entering their decline phase (2) … which adds to development costs and makes it hard to automate production processes (3). Longer life cycles make it easier to spread profits over the years (4) … putting less pressure on short-term profits (5).

Answering exams

It would be wise to expect regular exam questions on Product, innovation and the Product Life Cycle. Here are two possible exam questions; possible answers are on the right.

Q1. Which **one** of the following is an innovation?

A Designing the world's first robotic strawberry-picker

B Persuading Tesco to stock the UK's first alcoholic ice cream

C Thinking up a new way to iron shirts

D Writing a brilliant TV commercial

  (1 mark)

Q2. Evaluate whether or not Argos should spend extra to increase the speed of its home deliveries. (7 marks)

On the right are strong answers to these two questions.

Grade 9 Answers (Qs. on the left)

1. Answer B: *That's innovation (not invention)*

2. The case in favour of this is strong if research has shown speed of delivery to be very important to customers. To the customer, 'product' means everything involved in the purchase, including speed of delivery. If Argos can promise to deliver in an hour while rivals take a day or more, this could help Argos boost its market share without having to cut prices.

The case against this move, however, is that speed of delivery may bring only a very short-term advantage. It's too easily copied by others. Argos faces direct competitors such as John Lewis and the might of Amazon – so speedy delivery is unlikely to bring an advantage for long.

On balance, the case remains strong for the faster delivery because although it may not be an advantage for long, if we don't get there first, someone else will – leaving Argos behind.

Price

What? (Grade 5 basics)

Pricing strategies control the broad pricing decisions made by managers over the medium-long term. Arsenal season tickets, for example, have long been the most expensive in Europe.

When launching a new product, companies face a choice between three strategies:

- 'Skimming', which means pricing high to get high profit margins, even if sales volumes are fairly low
- 'Penetration', meaning to gain high volume sales by pricing low
- 'Competitor', meaning to price at the levels set by others already in the market

When the business is up and running there are two further pricing options: cost-plus pricing and promotional pricing.

> **Do** remember that the word strategy means medium-long term (the word 'tactic' is used for short-term thinking such as promotional pricing). So pricing strategies should run for years (or for ever in the case of Chanel No. 5 perfume).

Why? (Grade 6)

The value of a clear pricing strategy is that customers can get used to it. Arsenal supporters may grumble, but learn to accept the price of their support. Fans of Primark will go out of their way to buy low-priced fashion. So the pricing approach becomes part of the brand image.

How? (Grade 7)

If a new product is to be launched, managers must get a clear idea of its target market and the potential competition. If the target market is young, fashion and trend-conscious adults, a skimming strategy (pricing high) may work well. Even more so if there's no direct competition. Careful market research is needed to get a clear understanding of the target customer – their habits, attitudes and spending power. Other influences on the choice of pricing approach include technology and the product life cycle.

> **Don't** assume that low prices are always a good thing. Companies need profits – and cutting prices can make the business unprofitable.

So? (Grade 8)

Even if a business has chosen a successful pricing strategy for the birth phase of a product's life cycle, it doesn't mean the strategy must always stay the same. A penetration strategy might have been right for the Nintendo Switch when launched in 2017. But its sales success may be so strong that a decision is taken later to push the price level up. So by the time it reaches its maturity phase, the pricing may have moved towards a skimming strategy.

Grade 9

A consistent medium-term strategy can establish a price as the 'right' one in the mind of customers. They can learn to believe that Chanel No 5 perfume is 'worth' £70 for 50ml, even though perfumes are quite cheap to produce. The worst approach to pricing is to be inconsistent, with high prices one week and deep price cuts the next. Customers learn to wait for the bargain prices – and lose their faith in the brand image.

> **Exam tip:** when reading about the business featured in the exam, think about whether you would set high or low prices for the product or service being described. Write your thoughts alongside the text.

Price: 5-step logic chain (necessary to get to the top response level)

Chain 1. A brand new, highly innovative product/service should have a skimming strategy (1) … allowing prices high enough to give strong profit margins (2) … which can help finance further development work to create even better products in future (3). In effect this has been Apple's approach with its iPhones (4) … creating a virtuous circle of great products …. strong prices … funding even better products … at even higher prices. (5)

Chain 2. A trained hairdresser may want open a store in their home town, even though there are already 8 established rivals (1) … forcing the new business to decide whether to price competitively or to undercut the others with penetration pricing (2). A decision to price similarly to competitors may make it a little harder to break in to the market (3) … but easier to make reasonable profits in the medium-long term (4) … as long as the hairdresser's talent keeps customers coming back (5).

Answering exam questions

Questions about pricing come up regularly on Business exams. In a single set of OCR's 'specimen' exam papers, the words price or pricing were mentioned 6 times in the mark scheme. This shows the importance of this topic. Here are two possible exam questions:

Q1. Explain one pricing strategy that might be successful for a new pizza delivery business. (3 marks)

Q2. Fender is a producer of expensive guitars used by stars such as Bruno Mars.

Analyse two benefits to Fender of charging high prices for its musical instruments. (6 marks)

On the right are strong answers to these two questions.

Grade 9 Answers (Qs on the left)

1. As there are lots of pizza delivery businesses in almost every town, penetration pricing would be best. It will enable the business to carve out a share of the market by undercutting the prices of rivals. Once established, it can push prices up a little.

2. Stars such as Bruno Mars probably want to use a guitar that is priced out of the reach of ordinary customers. It would reinforce the image of stardom to have an exclusive, special guitar. So pricing high should help in achieving consistent sales among a small niche market of professional musicians. This should provide enough revenue to cover costs and a large enough profit to finance the continuing growth of the business.

Like any other business, Fender would want to develop – perhaps into more technologically advanced guitars. Good profits based on high prices can enable it to do this. In turn, that will help to attract more professional musicians in future.

Section 2.4: The Marketing Mix

Promotion

What? (Grade 5 basics)

Promotion means all the ways in which a business tries to persuade customers to buy: either now or in the future. The key to long-term success is branding, usually backed by image-building advertising and/or sponsorship. To boost today's sales businesses use special offers at the point-of-sale, such as price reductions or free samples. Special offers can also be promoted cheaply by social media or radio - with every company hoping that their offer 'goes viral'. The key to success is selecting the right promotional strategy for the targeted segment.

> **Do** remember that promotion is expensive. A single 30 second TV commercial can cost £250,000 - and several are needed to make an impact

Why? (Grade 6)

The need to identify the appropriate promotion strategy is because there are huge costs involved. SpecSavers spends nearly £50 million a year on promotion in the UK alone. So advertising must be carefully targeted at the right audience. Every advertisement watched by someone with great eyesight is a waste of the company's money.

> **Don't** focus too much on special offers. Yes, they can boost sales, but just for a short time. Companies want sales to grow steadily over time

How? (Grade 7)

The first decision is whether to focus on long-term promotion of the brand, or boosting short-term sales. Then a decision is needed on whether to focus on traditional advertising such as TV, or digital advertising via Google or social media. But it all depends on how much the business can afford to spend. Small businesses with little to spend on promotion may simply put leaflets through doors locally.

So? (Grade 8)

As promotion is so expensive, targeted advertising online is very attractive to companies. Advertising for stairlifts only pops up in front of older internet surfers; advertising for Nike appears in front of sports-loving under-35s. The ability to learn about individuals' tastes – and to target them accordingly – makes digital advertising better value and less wasteful than TV commercials.

> **Exam tip:** when thinking about promotion, consider the link between the brand name and image and the way the product is advertised. With the best companies, they go together perfectly

Grade 9

Every, literally every, business will say that the best form of promotion is word-of-mouth (or the Twitter equivalent). In other words you want to give customers such a great experience that they come back – and recommend you to others. It's not only free advertising, it's also the most powerful type.

Promotion: 5-step logic chain (to get to the top level of response)

Chain 1. A new business may have very little money to promote their first product or shop (1) ... making it vital to target the right people cost-effectively (2). That may mean low-cost leaflets through letter boxes (3) ... or a big effort to create a social media presence (4) ... but the business must make every effort to turn customers into fans – as nothing is as cost-effective as word-of-mouth recommendation (5)

Chain 2. To build up its brand name Just-Eat spent heavily on posters and TV from early on (1) ... to help customers understand that the Just-Eat website was the place to look when hungry (2). Now the business uses online media rather more (3) ... to target fast-food-lovers and to inform existing customers of special offers (4). As a product life cycle develops the type of promotion can change. (5)

Place

What? (Grade 5 basics)

Place means the methods of distribution that get products from the factory to the consumer. This might be via physical or digital distribution channels. For a market-leading brand such as Heinz Beans, getting and keeping distribution is not hard – every grocery shop wants Heinz on the shelf. But for lesser brands such as Branston Beans or for a brand new producer, Place can be a huge problem, i.e. persuading shops to find shelf-space for your product.

Why? (Grade 6)

Whereas online 'digital' retailers can locate warehouses where rents are low, physical shops need to be where people go – where rents are expensive. So shops have to keep stocked with high-selling products, and are wary of taking a risk with a new, unknown brand. If it sells badly it's a waste of valuable, costly shelf-space.

How? (Grade 7)

To persuade shops to stock your product you need to offer good credit terms ('please buy 20 packs today – we'll wait 2 months before sending the bill') and a big discount off the retail price. The shopkeeper needs to make a profit. Strong established brands are in a much stronger position, and will offer lower discounts and shorter credit periods.

So? (Grade 8)

For new businesses, Place is often the most difficult of the '4Ps'. Just at the time the business is shortest of cash, shopkeepers demand long credit terms – and big discounts off the price. And even when you've managed to sell to a retailer such as Sainsbury's, the shop managers demand that you meet ambitious sales targets – otherwise the product gets 'de-listed', i.e. withdrawn from the shelves and sent back to the factory.

Grade 9

There are lots of reasons why digital, online retailing can be more profitable than a high-street shop with a big rent bill and big local business taxes. But physical distribution can still be important. Superdry wants to show you its full range of products in the setting it has chosen for itself. Then you may decide to buy online from Superdry.com. So today's shops can be showrooms as well as taking in cash.

> **Do** think about the difference between physical and digital retailing. More than 25% of clothes are now bought online – and well over 50% of books.

> **Don't** doubt the power of retailers such as Tesco. Recently they've been refusing to stock products even from major producers such as Pepsi. Keeping your place can be as hard as getting it.

> **Exam tip:** examiners like you to be aware that place is nothing without profit. So it is not worth slashing your prices just to get distribution. Better to be in 50 shops profitably than 500 unprofitably.

Place: 5-step logic chain (to get to the top level of response)

Chain 1. A business with a good product that struggles to get distribution might build a website for digital sales (1) … thereby keeping the profit margin that used to be taken by the shops (2). The extra profit can be used to build up the website to make it better and better (as ASOS has done over the years) (3) … and to promote the site using social media (4). Therefore make it the best Place for buying online (5).

Chain 2. For a new business offering an innovative new product (1) … it should be possible to persuade trendy shops to try it out (2). The problem then is to persuade enough customers to buy that the shops keep the product in distribution (3). This is easier if the shops give the product a great display space, such as next to the checkout (4). They'll be willing to do that if they get a generous discount off the price, and therefore a big profit margin (5).

Marketing Mix and Making Decisions

What? (Grade 5 basics)

There are two key issues here: the importance of pulling the 4 elements of the mix together to make a coherent strategy; and using the mix to build a strong, successful business. Business decisions might include finding the right marketing mix to challenge a successful rival; or changing the mix when the life cycle moves from growth to maturity.

Why? (Grade 6)

Ultimately, business is about making decisions. Not all will be right, but a manager who gets two thirds right can probably sleep securely. As all business decisions are about the future, the results are always uncertain. So an intelligently planned marketing mix may prove unsuccessful – there's no shame in that. Where there should be shame is when the mix is poorly coordinated, leaving customers and staff unsure of the product's image and credibility.

How? (Grade 7)

Start with careful market research; make a clear decision about the target market segment – then build a well-planned marketing mix focused on that target. This is how Nintendo's Switch became a success – by targeting customers other than the core market young, male fans of PS4 or Xbox One.

So? (Grade 8)

Business is not about quick wins, it's about building something. ASOS was floated on the stock market in 2001 for 20p. In February 2018 the shares were over £70. Someone who had invested £1,000 in 2001 would have had £350,000 by 2018. ASOS established itself by being first into the online fashion clothing business – and sustained their advantage over newcomers. Marketing decisions that lead to long-term success can be worth a fortune.

Grade 9

Gaining an advantage over your rivals is difficult; sustaining it for years is even harder. Jealous rivals copy what's working for you – so the only way to stay ahead is to keep innovating. The ASOS website today is a brilliant development on the past, making full use of social media and the development of a Selfie culture. Getting ahead is clever; staying ahead is brilliant.

> **Do** show your understanding that marketing must be based on consumer wants and needs. A well-thought-out marketing mix points the product in the right direction, backed by the other 3 mix elements.

> **Don't** wreck an answer by pulling one element of the mix away from the rest. If the product and promotion are stylish and classy, don't suggest a bargain price!

> **Exam tip:** the marketing mix helps managers put decisions into practice. Once Elon Musk launches the first Tesla self-drive car, a marketing manager will decide on price, promotion and place.

The Mix and Decisions: 5-step logic chain (getting to the top response level)

Chain 1. To stop sales sliding for Kellogg's Special K a new strategy is needed (1) … by changing the image to focus on 'special', e.g. 'Special K – for when you've done something special' (2). This changes the promotional message (3) … and perhaps the pack design should have some gold as well as red (4). A well-integrated marketing mix could help Special K sales move forward again (5).

Chain 2. Faced with whether to launch a new product that has shone in research (1) … a key issue is if all 4 elements of the marketing mix point firmly towards the target customers (2). If one element looks weak the whole package may fail (3). If that one problem can be overcome, perhaps by going online (4) … it should be possible to build a solid market share for the business (5).

Answering exams

OCR produces sample exam papers to help teachers. In these there is one question directly about the marketing mix. But in OCR's marking guidance there are plenty of mentions of the mix as a way of answering other questions.

Here are 3 questions where the mix and is being tested:

Q1. Analyse how a small business could market its product despite having a small budget. (3 marks)

Q2 Analyse how the proposed changes to Shirtz Ltd's marketing mix might impact on two stakeholder groups.

Stakeholder group 1

Stakeholder group 2

(6 marks)

Q3. Discuss whether a business can succeed if its marketing mix is poorly integrated. (6)

On the right are strong answers to these three questions. They are models for writing about the topic rather than models for how to score 6 marks.

Grade 9 Answers (see questions on the left)

Q1. It must keep its spending low by taking care over every element of its marketing mix. Promotional spending must be very low (online only?) and distribution ('place') kept to high volume, low-priced distributors.

Q2. Stakeholder group 1 is the company's two full-time production workers. The plan for growth should excite the two, though staff are often fearful of new machinery. In this case, as long as the plan succeeds in boosting demand, the staff's jobs should be very safe.

Stakeholder group 2 is the company's customers. Once money has been spent expanding the business it may be necessary to cut the price back a little to encourage higher demand. This use of the marketing mix should lead to Shirtz attracting new customers to the business.

Q3. If the mix is poorly integrated it will always be difficult for customers to understand the marketing and branding. Mercedes might have a wonderful Product at a high Price and distributed in the right (posh) Place, but if it ran a Buy One Get One Free promotion on the cars, the image would be wrecked.

However, if the business has no rivals, this may hardly matter, e.g. Tesla cars, before any other producer made an exciting, expensive electric car. So yes, a business can succeed for a while even if its marketing mix is poorly integrated, but when serious competition arrives it will have to rethink its marketing strategy and mix.

Interpretation of market data

What? (Grade 5 basics)

To judge the effectiveness of a company's marketing, lots of number-crunching is involved. Important data includes changes in demand (sales), changes in market share and calculating the effects on sales of spending on promotion. Business want an answer to the question: Do we get value for money for what we spend on marketing?

Why? (Grade 6)

There is no doubt that chocolate producers need to spend money on cocoa, sugar, milk and packaging materials. And no doubt that they need a factory, production staff and vans to deliver the product. But there's always a question mark over how much should be spent on marketing. The giant Unilever spends more than £6,000 million (£6bn) each year on 'brand and marketing investment'. It would love to cut that figure if it could. So careful measurement of the effectiveness of marketing spending is essential.

How? (Grade 7)

To calculate changes in demand, it may be necessary to work out the percentage change. This is done using the formula: Change/Original x 100. To work out market share requires the calculation: One company's sales/All the sales in a market x 100. In both cases, see the calculations on the right.

So? (Grade 8)

Some of the most successful businesses succeed without spending a penny on advertising, for example Tesla Motors. Such is the love for these electric cars that media mentions of the products are enough to promote them. But when a business such as Unilever spends £6 billion on marketing, any opportunity to spend less could boost the company's profits hugely. And it could spend less if only it could make its spending more effective, e.g. cleverer, more memorable advertisements and stronger brand names and reputations.

Grade 9

Companies collect market data all the time. If one brand is booming while another has poor sales, managers want to know. They may be able to squeeze extra profit from the success and find a way to rebuild sales of the struggler. As profit is the ultimate measure of success, managing the sales and revenue numbers is critical.

> **Change in demand:** if last year's sales were 2,400 units and this year's are 3,000, the change is +600. And the % change is =600/2,400 x 100 = **+25%**

> **Market share** if your company sales are 3,000 units and total sales in the market are 50,000 units, you have a market share of 3,000/50,000 x 100 = **6%**.

> **Exam tip:** examiners like to see that you understand the importance of numbers in business – and also understand that numbers are hard to predict, e.g. next year's sales or market share. Business is about estimates and good judgement.

Interpretation of market data: 5-step logic chain (for the top level of response)

Chain 1. A great starting point for a new business is to estimate the total size of a market (1) ... such as that spending on chocolate in the UK is about £3.5 billion a year (2). This allows a calculation such as 'If we could get a 1% market share we'd have £35 million of sales' (3) ... and then think how that could be achieved profitably (4)... perhaps by supplying own label chocolates to Marks & Spencer (5).

Chain 2. It's hard to estimate the effect of marketing spending on the level of sales (1) ... but it can be done if you carefully measure market share figures (2)... before, during and after your marketing campaign (3). The only problem might be if your competitors choose to run an important marketing effort themselves (4)... for example their cut-price offer might dent your sales and market share (5).

The purpose of human resources in business

What? (Grade 5 basics)

Despite the talk of robots and artificial intelligence, people remain the heart of every business. Many a company says that 'our people are our greatest asset'. This is obvious for service businesses such as cafés, where a warm smile and a smiley face in the coffee froth adds to customer satisfaction. In product development and production people are also vital: they come up with the innovative new ideas; their motivation helps boost productivity.

Why? (Grade 6)

So why call people 'human resources'? It's a horrible term, implying that people are 'resources' – to be bought and sold in the same way that a business might buy new equipment or packaging. It's the right term for a business such as Amazon, which treats warehouse staff as hourly-paid robots. But it shouldn't be used by a business that values its people – and wants to see staff build successful careers.

How? (Grade 7)

The purpose of people in business organisations is to help generate and fulfil customer orders. In other words turn customer needs and wants into profitable sales that create sufficient customer satisfaction to make the customer come back for more. This can be done by well-trained, well-motivated staff willing to take the initiative to help a potential customer become an actual, satisfied one.

So? (Grade 8)

It's hard to get ahead and keep ahead in business; many things can go wrong that are out of management's hands – such as a sudden fall in consumer spending due to rising unemployment. But one thing managers can control is the quality and effectiveness of staff. They must recruit well, give excellent training and find a way to get staff to commit to – and stay with – the business. Top level human resource management goes a long way towards success for the business as a whole.

Grade 9

Some businesses see staff as a cost, to be screwed down as low as possible. Others see staff as an asset, to be proud of, to develop and to value for the long term. Those seeing staff as 'resources', with costs to be minimised, don't worry about keeping people for the long term. For the employee, it's hugely better to work for a company that cares about the long-term future for their staff. In the long-run, it's also better for the company to have high staff loyalty and retention.

> **Do** remember that businesses don't simply want to make staff 'happy' – they want to make a profit from the work that staff do. But this doesn't mean you have to cut wages to the minimum. Well-paid, well-motivated staff can come up with new ideas to make business boom.

> **Don't** muddle motivation with productivity. Well motivated staff may not be any more productive, but enthusiasm and commitment can give customers a better experience – and bring them back.

> **Exam tip**: work hard to distinguish recruitment from selection, job roles from responsibility and so on. In other words take care over the language of people in business

---

Ways of working: 5-step logic chain (to get to top level of response)

Chain 1. Identifying what the business needs from its people may be harder than it sounds (1) ... because companies are changing constantly, e.g. due to new technology (2). The best companies know that the future is uncertain, and therefore develop the ability of staff to adapt (3)... perhaps by training them in a wide range of skills (4) ... going some way to making their people future-proof. (5)

Chain 2. Meeting what the business needs from its staff can be expensive (1) ... as training not only costs money but also requires staff to be absent from work during the training sessions (2). So the business must spend today for benefits in the future (3) ... which may be difficult if finances are tight (4) ... but if top managers are really committed to staff development, they'll probably find a way. (5)

Organisational structures

What? (Grade 5 basics)

The plan of who is answerable to whom in a business is known as the organisational structure. It sets out the layers of management, starting with the Chief Executive and going down to the 'shopfloor'. In a standard organisational structure, every individual down a chain of command is the subordinate of a single boss. A well-run business makes sure that responsible tasks are delegated to junior staff.

Why? (Grade 6)

There may be little need for a formal hierarchy in a small business, where everyone knows who manages whom. But in a massive business such as Tesco, with more than 250,000 staff, it can be helpful to see who is answerable to whom. If a young member of staff feels bullied by their supervisor, it's helpful to find out the supervisor's boss – to go to make a complaint. Then the bullying will stop. It's also great for junior staff to see the 'career ladder' – the promotion opportunities that may come their way in future.

How? (Grade 7)

To set out the structure, there are two factors to consider: the vertical structure, e.g. how many management layers are there to be; and the horizontal structure, e.g. how many supervisors will be managed directly by a single boss (known as the 'span of control'). In some companies the average boss may be in charge of 4 people; in others the boss may have 8 or 9 under their control – a much bigger challenge.

So? (Grade 8)

In some businesses the hierarchy is flat, in other words not many layers of management. Each manager needs to be responsible for many junior staff (perhaps 10-12) because no supervisors are employed. This forces managers to trust their juniors, because they haven't got time to check up on everybody, all the time. In other companies the structure is tall, with a narrow span of control.

Grade 9

In 'centralised' organisations, bosses keep all the decision-making at the top of the hierarchy. Juniors are told what to do. In 'decentralised' organisations, many decisions are passed down to junior staff, to encourage them to get involved in management – and to find out which juniors deserve to be promoted. So organisational structure has a major impact on staff motivation.

> **Do** consider which structure is most appropriate for the business in question. If the market is young and fast-growing, a flat structure will encourage fast decision-making by junior staff.

> **Don't** assume there's one best organisational structure. It depends on the business. Young, growing businesses thrive on decentralised, flat structures. Older companies tend to develop tall hierarchies.

> **Exam tip:** remember that a flat hierarchy works well with a decentralised approach. A taller hierarchy is likely to lead to a more centralised approach, keeping decisions at the top.

Organisational structure: 5-step logic chain (to get to the top level of response)

Chain 1. If a large business is struggling with market share it might consider a flatter organisational structure (1) ... to encourage younger staff to come up with new ideas (2) ... that may turn into profitable new products (3) When decisions are centralised at the top (4) ... they reflect the views of older, wealthy managers; those nearer the shopfloor are more tuned into ordinary people's tastes (5)

Chain 2. When a business has a highly profitable, stable brand it focuses on keeping things that way (1) ... and therefore focuses on avoiding mistakes (2). Therefore power is held at the top (3) ... and a tall hierarchy makes sure all ideas are checked by superiors (4) ... whose job is to avoid mistakes (5)

Terminology of Organisation Charts

What? (Grade 5 basics)

Organisation charts who is answerable to whom. From the top to bottom of the organisation there will be a **chain of command** that shows how the most junior staff member is ultimately answerable to the business leader. This chain helps in the process of **delegation**, in other words passing authority down the hierarchy. A person in **authority** (has power over others) can delegate some of that authority to **subordinates** (more junior staff). Having been given authority, the subordinates can make decisions. Each boss has a **span of control** which measures the number of subordinates who the boss controls directly. The wider the span, the more staff are answerable to that boss.

Why? (Grade 6)

Precise language prevents waffle. It takes a lot of waffly words to explain 'wide span of control' or 'long chain of command'. Students who can quickly and correctly use business terms impress the examiners and avoid wasting time. And, later, it helps in job interviews if you can talk the language of business.

How? (Grade 7)

To use the terminology effectively, it's good to practise the main ways each term is used. For span of control the key measures are wide versus narrow. With a narrow span the manager has only perhaps 2 or 3 staff answerable directly to that boss. A chain of command will be quite short in a flat hierarchy where there are few layers between top and bottom. In a tall hierarchy the chain of command will be long.

So? (Grade 8)

Top candidates can not only use terms in the right way, but also see their implications. Pretty obviously, in a huge business with a tall hierarchy, the chain of command may be so long (let's say 24 layers from top to bottom) that it may take crazily long for an idea from the shopfloor to reach the overall boss. Clever businesses see the problem, and work hard to tackle it – especially if the people on the shopfloor have daily contact with customers – and therefore know how to make the company's products adapt to changing customer tastes/fashions.

Grade 9

With terminology, don't wait to be asked for it. Spot the opportunity to turn a vague point into something more specific and more sophisticated. Grade 9 answers are full of terms such as span of control – used relevantly and correctly.

> **Do** be brave in using business terminology – especially in class and home-work. Your teacher will spot when you haven't quite understood a word – and set you straight

> **Don't** misuse the term 'delegation'. People seem to think it means telling juniors what to do. It doesn't. It means passing authority (power) down to subordinates, e.g. decision-making power over hiring new staff

> **Exam tip**: examiners like to test words that have a specific meaning – and they love the topic of organisational structures. So do make sure to learn all the terms on this section of the specification

---

Organisational terminology: 5-step logic chain (to get top level of response)

Chain 1. If a business has been slow to adapt to new customer tastes, perhaps its chain of command is too long (1) ... resulting in few if any thoughts from the shopfloor reaching the Directors (2) ... and those that do arrive may get there too late (3). So the business should consider cutting the management layers (4) ... leading to wider spans of control but also faster vertical communication (5)

Chain 2. Some people in authority find it hard to delegate effectively (1) ... perhaps because they don't trust their subordinates' judgement (2). Therefore they keep hold of power (3) ... only delegating unimportant decisions (4) ... frustrating ambitious staff who want to show their skills (5)

Ways of Working

What? (Grade 5 basics)

Although people may think of a working life being based on a permanent, full-time job, there are other ways to work. Some part-timers have regular hours, such as 10.00 – 3.00 weekdays, so that kids can be taken to school. Others have irregular hours, flexible hours dictated by the employer. One week there's 20 hours' work, the next week nothing. This is OK for a young adult living at home, but not for a parent trying to pay regular bills such as the rent.

Why? (Grade 6)

Many businesses want a flexible workforce. Permanent, full-time staff work 35 hours when it's busy and 35 hours when things are slack. An efficient business wants to match working hours to the work needed. An ice cream factory may need to work 24/7 from May to August, but only for 5 hours a day in January and February. So the business may employ just a quarter of staff as permanent, full-timers and the remainder flexibly. Some temporary staff on 6-month contracts for the summer plus daily contract staff for when the weather's exceptional.

How? (Grade 7)

In the past, job contracts were pieces of paper setting out the hours and length of service. Now technology helps with more flexible arrangements. Working from home once risked losing contact with what's going on, but e-mail and Facetime now make it easy to avoid the boring commute. And Uber's App allows its drivers to log in or out at any time, providing flexibility for the business and the staff.

So? (Grade 8)

In an ideal world, the requirements of workers would be matched by the offers available from employers. Many people need the security of full-time, permanent jobs – but sometimes there aren't enough available. Perhaps more companies should care about hiring and keeping great people, and slightly less about flexibility. It may help those businesses have more motivated, more engaged staff.

Grade 9

In Business exams it's no problem to suggest that ethics should be a higher priority than profit. It's also reasonable to say that providing what staff need may boost morale and motivation. So why not let a parent go part-time, or give a young person wanting their first mortgage the chance of a full-time, permanent job? It may add to short-term costs, but build a more loyal workforce in the long term.

> **Do** take care over the difference between flexible work and self-employment. Flexible working still means being an employee. It therefore still has some security. Self-employment means you're running your own, one-person business

> **Don't** doubt the importance of technology, not just for remote working but also the speed and efficiency with which Apps can match people to the jobs that need to be done. The Uber approach may be the future.

> **Exam tip:** write about people at work with care and compassion. Some students write as if hiring and firing staff is natural - not a problem. Well, it is.

Ways of working: 5-step logic chain (to get to top level of response)

Chain 1. Many businesses have seasonal demand and therefore can't be efficient if everyone is on a permanent contract (1) ... so there is a proper business case for flexible working (2). Some businesses seize the opportunity to create a job in which holiday pay and pensions don't need to be paid for (3)... which seems like exploitation (4). Trade union membership is one way staff can protect themselves (5)

Chain 2. Flexible contracts can be great for young people (1) ... especially if they can work long hours one week, then take the next week off (2). So flexible working isn't all bad (3) ... especially if there's flexibility on both sides (4). What feels wrong is a situation where the flexibility works really well for the business, but at the expense of the security of a family. (5)

Communications in Business

What? (Grade 5 basics)

In a small business, everyone chats and everyone knows what's going on. So if the boss is out, others can help customers with a problem – or help clients wanting to place a big order. In large businesses this is harder, especially if many staff are part-timers or temporary. So communication is an issue – and often a problem. Some people believe email and texts have made things worse, with too few face-to-face meetings, and too many messages sent that are of no interest to many. But few would doubt the rising importance of digital communications on business activity.

Why? (Grade 6)

The problem in a big business is there's so much going on that most people can only tune in to a small part. If I'm in charge of fresh fruit for Sainsbury in Northampton, I may only be interested in my store plus the category I'm working in. So general emails flood into my Inbox – but leave me cold. Clever communication makes sure people only need to think about the things that matter to them.

How? (Grade 7)

The solution is to be selective. Too much communication is tough to wade through. But cutting back too much might mean a key message is missed. So bosses must make sure individuals only receive the information needed to do their job well. Even if the right messages are getting through, there can still be barriers to effective communication. Top bosses may use business-speak that junior staff can't follow.

So? (Grade 8)

It is important that top bosses see the value of effective communications throughout the business. Staff should be told that top bosses like to hear from the shopfloor, and middle managers should know never to block a message. And with electronic communication, selectivity is all-important.

Grade 9

In small businesses communication may be so easy and natural that no-one knows it can be 'a problem'. In bigger businesses it should always be on the mind of managers and bosses alike. Find a way to overcome communication barriers and you're a big step forward to being successful. Digital communications seem to be of help, but email inboxes may get so crowded that they harm productivity.

> **Do** think about the influence of digital communication on modern businesses. Some are inherently one-way, such as a website; others are two-way such as texts and social media, so they give feedback

> **Don't** forget that old-style communications still has a place. A letter is a great way to impress a potential employer or customer; and effective speaking in a meeting or a presentation can also be impressive

> **Exam tip:** Good communication doesn't mean lots of it. Show the examiner you understand how people today can get flooded with emails, perhaps struggling to focus on the important parts of their job.

Communication in Business: 5-step logic chain (to get to top level of response)

Chain 1. To give better customer service it's important to improve communications (1) … because a customer message that fails to get through can mean the wrong delivery is made (2) … wasting the company's money and the customer's time (3). This might end up with the customer looking elsewhere (4) … and finding a new, more efficient supplier that they choose to stay with (5).

Chain 2. Many businesses have their factory in one part of the country and the Headquarters somewhere else (usually London) (1) … which makes communication mistakes especially likely (2). So regular, face-to-face meetings are needed (3) … as it would be reckless to rely purely on email (4) … as so many staff complain that their Inboxes are too full to pick out the few important messages. (5)

Recruitment Methods

What? (Grade 5 basics)

Before recruiting, businesses must identify the job roles and responsibilities they need. Directors may be in place, but as the business expands they may need a new layer of senior managers. These new roles need to be created to help make future plans successful. When recruiting senior managers, the business may look for internal candidates or for people outside the business (external recruitment).

Why? (Grade 6)

Effective recruitment needs a clear idea about the personal qualities needed by staff in different job roles. Company directors need the experience and talent to make decisions about the long-term future of the business. Managers, team leaders and supervisors need to be able to organise and motivate staff towards the achievement of clear targets. And operational and support staff need to work hard and intelligently, but under the direction of their supervisors.

How? (Grade 7)

Having identified the need for a new recruit, two documents are needed. A job description sets out the tasks and responsibilities of the job; and a person specification identifies the qualifications, experience and personality of the ideal recruit. Applicants for the job will need to fill out an application form and provide a C.V. – a written statement by each candidate about their background, achievements and ambitions. Then the selection process can take place.

So? (Grade 8)

If you run a business that is growing well and making good profits, it makes sense to recruit internally. The person who already works for you knows and understands the business – and will therefore be able to work well straight away. And internal promotions help motivate other staff – and make them less likely to look for jobs elsewhere. Whereas businesses in crisis are likely to look outside – for an external candidate with fresh ideas.

Grade 9

So, depending on the business situation, you might either recommend a search for someone completely new – who can shake things up and force existing staff to re-think their attitudes and behaviours. Or recommend an internal candidate who can keep the ship sailing steadily on the same course. It depends on the circumstances of the business at that time (which you get from the text).

> **Do** think about recruitment from the point of view of the business. Companies want people who are reliable, keen, willing to learn and work well with others.

> **Don't** forget why businesses recruit: to replace employees who leave, to help cope with business growth and to fill any skill gaps that emerge – perhaps when technology is moving ahead sharply.

> **Exam tip**: examiners ask a lot of questions about internal & external recruitment. Prepare by thinking about two or three of your favourite – and least favourite – shops. Should they be recruiting externally? Why, exactly?

Recruitment methods: 5-step logic chain (to get to top level of response)

Chain 1. SuperDry has been expanding steadily and successfully using internal recruitment (1) … for all jobs above the shopfloor level, such as supervisors and managers (2). This helps in developing a consistent way of working throughout management (3) … which in turn makes it easier for supervisors to become managers (4). For new shopfloor staff, external recruitment is needed (5).

Chain 2. To be effective, recruitment must lead to the right type of people being hired (1) … such as outgoing, friendly staff to work in a coffee shop or bar (2). Happy, chatty staff boosts customer service (3) … which can lead to more customer loyalty/repeat business (4) … boosting the company's revenue and profits. (5)

Methods of selection

What? (Grade 5 basics)

A lot is needed to get a good range of the right people applying for a job. Once that's been achieved, the key is to get the selection process right: choosing the best person from the available candidates. The single most common selection method is the interview – these days often by phone or Skype. Other important methods are CVs, a letter of application, tests, group activities and references.

Why? (Grade 6)

Making the right selection is hugely important, especially in a small business. If only four people work in a business, hiring the fifth may enrich the working life of all, or may poison it. This is why people tend to recruit new staff who have similar characteristics to those who already work in the business. This is understandable, but may be the cause of discrimination by race, gender or social background.

How? (Grade 7)

A decision is needed about which selection methods should be used. Typically, the more important the hiring decision, the more complex the methods. So full-day group activities (problem-solving and perhaps team-based) are used to hire graduate management trainees. Shop-floor staff may get little more than a phone interview and a check on references. The methods chosen should also reflect the skills required. For a trainee accountant a maths test may be sensible, whereas someone a receptionist should be interviewed face-to-face to assess personality and warmth.

So? (Grade 8)

All the evidence is that selection is riddled with discrimination problems. At interview, managers tend to choose people like them – similar school, similar social background and so on. And with references it's easy for former bosses to think in stereotypes. Modern managers have to keep thinking of the benefits to the business of having a better, fuller racial, social and gender mix in the workforce.

Grade 9

The best selection process has a balance between relatively objective measures such as a maths test and the far more judgemental ones such as an interview or group activities. The key is always to get the best person for the job. The best choice may not fit easily within the group, but still be too good to turn down. As long as the existing staff get on well together, they should cope with the change.

> **Do** remember that hiring the wrong person is costly. It means poor productivity, perhaps a hit to the team spirit, and the cost of going through the recruitment process again

> **Don't** forget the business context, i.e. the business story the exam board has written. A successful business may be right to choose someone just like the existing staff. A struggling one may need someone quite different.

> **Exam tip**: make sure to separate recruitment from selection. Recruitment is deciding who to recruit and getting applicants interested. Selection means choosing the best of the candidates.

Recruitment methods: 5-step logic chain (to get to top level of response)

Chain 1. When selecting new staff it's sensible to be cautious about all the information provided (1) … from the CV (better check the accuracy) to the references (it may be truth, but is it the whole truth?) (2). Today's recruit may end up as tomorrow's leader (3) … perhaps facing greater scrutiny from the press media (4) … and no-one wants the embarrassment of a 'degree' that wasn't (5).

Chain 2. In fast-moving businesses such as high-tech start-ups selection is especially important (1) … because getting the brightest people is the key to better innovation (2) … which in turn can mean rising market share and rising profitability (3). In this case informal processes may work well, such as chatting about the applicant's personal projects(4)… which may show the skills the company needs (5)

Motivation and retention

What? (Grade 5 basics)

Staff motivation is important to keep productivity and retention high. It also helps in attracting top young talent, if word spreads that this is a great place to work. Motivation comes about when individuals feel confident that their abilities and achievements are recognised. So managers have a big role to play: to give staff a task with enough challenge for their talents to show through – and then to see who's rising to that challenge.

Why? (Grade 6)

Many managers think it's enough for staff to give 'a fair day's work for a fair day's pay'. But – just like school students – most staff could put twice as much effort and thought into their work, if they really wanted to. Motivated staff do exactly that. They don't work down to the average effort involved in a 'fair day's work', they do their best. Just like the footballer who gives '110%' and clearly just loves playing. There are few more important topics in business than human motivation.

There's also the important topic of retention, in other words staff staying rather than leaving for a job elsewhere. High staff retention keeps avoids the awful situation at a school where GCSE students have had 5 maths teachers in the past 2 years.

How? (Grade 7)

Businesses 'motivate' employees in two ways. Most of the ways used by managers aren't really about motivation at all – they are about incentives. Financial incentives include pay, bonuses, profit sharing, the promise of promotion and fringe benefits such as a company car. These forms of financial reward provide a target that many staff will try to achieve. To motivate staff, though, it's better to create a more interesting, challenging job by delegating authority over decision making. A further non-financial approach is praise as part of a healthy, positive working environment.

So? (Grade 8)

If you look at the difference between Number 1 and Number 2 in the Premier League or in cafes in your High Street, the explanation is often motivation. Not that staff are paid more, but because they care more – they have a passion and therefore an energy that has been turned into success. This can be due to an inspirational leader: an Elon Musk or a Pep Guardiola, but is often because staff have been given authority, and trusted by being given responsibility.

Grade 9

Years ago business was largely about manufacturing. So motivation mattered most in terms of productivity: making 20 chocolate bars a minute instead of 16. Today 80% of the UK economy is based on services: from making TV programmes to selling clothes in-store or online. So a vital part of motivation today is getting great, creative ideas from staff. You want them feeling involved enough to pass on ideas to their bosses. Japanese car giant Toyota is resisting the move to robot production because they value staff ideas too much to replace staff with robots.

Do remember the short list of benefits from motivation identified by OCR:
- improved employee performance,
- helps employee retention

Don't confuse production and productivity. Production means counting the amount produced in a day or week. Productivity is different: it measures efficiency, e.g. output per person per hour.

Exam tip 1: examiners love business words, so learn the definition of 'retention', 'productivity', 'authority' and 'fringe benefits'.

Exam tip 2: If you can link motivation to productivity, it's easy then to relate it to keeping costs down and therefore gaining an advantage over competitors.

Motivation and retention: 5-step logic chain (getting to the top response level)

Chain 1. When a bright new manager gives staff more authority and responsibility (1) … it can spark a boost to productivity (2) … which helps bring costs per unit down and efficiency up (3) … which makes the business more competitive (4) … which may help it succeed not only in the UK but also in overseas markets (5).

Chain 2. The super-successful businesses such as Google pay great salaries with amazing fringe benefits (1) … not to motivate staff but to retain them (2) … and to attract the best and brightest from the best universities (3). For motivation they rely on providing junior staff with authority for the work itself (4) … giving staff the opportunity to make their name with a brilliant new product idea. (5).

Answering exams

Here are 3 questions where motivation is being tested. All are written in the OCR style:

Q1. Explain one reason why a business may decide to pay its workers a bonus. (2)

Q2. Explain one drawback to a business of not being able to retain its employees. (2)

Q3. Tesco wants to improve staff motivation. It sees two options: Option 1 is to use non-financial methods and Option 2 is to use financial methods.

Justify which one of these two options you recommend. (9)

On the right are strong answers to these three questions. They are models for writing about the topic rather than models for how to score 3 or 9 marks.

Grade 9 Answers (questions on left)

Q1. It may pay a bonus in order to focus staff on a key objective, such as cutting food wastage. Achieving this will cut variable costs and therefore cut the break-even point – as long as the bonus isn't too big.

Q2. When a new member of staff starts, it takes many weeks to reach full effectiveness. At the start they're asking more questions than doing anything useful. If you can't retain your employees you keep needing to hire new staff. And their inefficiency would hit productivity.

Q3. To motivate staff non-financial methods should be chosen. Tesco wants enthusiastic staff who are helpful to customers, so delegation and praise are the way forward. This would give staff a greater sense of responsibility and commitment – hopefully commitment to customers' needs and wants.

On the other hand staff at Tesco may be so used to doing the same low-level tasks day-in day-out that they may be worried, even stressed, by being offered more responsibility. In the long term delegation and praise may be the way forward, but perhaps in the short term it would be disruptive – causing a jolt to labour retention.

Tesco should test out any changes in one or two stores before deciding what to do next.

Financial & non-financial methods of motivation

What? (Grade 5 basics)

Financial incentives can motivate staff to work harder. These include bonuses, profit sharing and fringe benefits – on top of normal pay. In the modern world, though, working harder may not be enough. Working smarter may be more important, for instance to come up with better ways of doing things. For this you need staff motivated generally, i.e. who want the business to do well. Non-financial methods help in this, such as praise, award schemes and a positive and pleasant working environment.

Why? (Grade 6)

Years ago, business success came from getting staff to do the same thing – faster. Today it's about finding different, better ways to do things. In the end, people will always be beaten by robots if the task remains unchanged for years. So innovation is needed not only in the products being made, but also in how to make them.

How? (Grade 7)

Companies tend to separate out the financial from the non-financial methods of motivation. Some businesses set up work tasks so that they can be learnt easily and done repeatedly – in return for high pay for those who work super-hard. Other managements encourage staff to come up with their own way to do things, providing praise and encouragement for those with good ideas.

So? (Grade 8)

The best teacher isn't always the hardest-worker. She may have skills backed by a personality that brings the subject to life. So financial rewards aimed at working harder may be irrelevant. Exam success comes from reading the examiner's text with care, and drawing conclusions about the business in question. Yes, if the company makes jeans it may make sense to pay workers per pair produced. But in service businesses (including teaching), non-financial methods are more important.

Grade 9

Motivation is a hugely important subject. In a tough world, it can be the difference between success and collapse. So it's vital for human resource managers to make the right decisions about how to motivate. Your teachers could offer you a bonus (£10?) for doing your homework, but would you do your best? Or just do well enough to get the tenner? Praise and encouragement, plus good training/teaching, may be a better to way to get you to give of your best.

> **Do** distinguish between the financial methods. Bonuses are usually a result of the individual worker's efforts, but profit-sharing gives everyone the same % bonus based on the success of the whole business. It's more of a thank-you than an incentive.

> **Don't** muddle bonuses with award schemes. In this case 'award' means something like a prize (Best Salesperson in Scotland) that may have no money attached to it. Good for the ego, not the bank balance.

> **Exam tip:** always relate motivation to retention. Good companies need loyal staff, so high retention is a huge target – and helped a lot by motivation.

Ways of working: 5-step logic chain (to get to top level of response)

Chain 1. Motivating staff by financial methods needs a good understanding of how those staff work and think (1) ... because some like to work individually, getting a bonus based on personal effort (2) ... whereas others like to work together as a team (3)... getting a profit share in the same way as staff at John Lewis/Waitrose (4). But such bonuses need to be high enough to matter, e.g. 15% of salary. (5)

Chain 2. Motivating by non-financial methods can help with productivity (1) ... but may have even more impact on retention (2). For example a nicer working environment (better canteen etc) doesn't motivate, but does give a strong reason to stay (3) ... which helps cut recruitment costs which should pay for the better facilities(4)...helping the business without risking damage to profitability. (5)

Importance of Employee Retention

What? (Grade 5 basics)

Employee retention measures the percentage of staff that stay, e.g. retention this year is 82% - down on last year's 85%. So this year 18% of the workforce left. The higher the retention figure, the fewer the number of new staff needing to be recruited and trained. Even beyond their training period new staff may be ineffective until they've got to know the customers and know which suppliers can be trusted and which ones need careful checking.

Why? (Grade 6)

Employee retention is important because key staff often have vital knowledge of how parts of the business work. For example if the IT manager leaves a school it may be hard for the replacement to understand details of the computer network. Specialist staff may also leave a business with some hugely important secrets that rival companies would be thrilled to have. High retention helps to stop secrets leaking away.

How? (Grade 7)

To achieve a high level of retention, staff must be paid well enough to stop them looking elsewhere and feel content not only with their current working life but also their future prospects. A chance of promotion or a chance of new exciting challenges helps to keep staff loyal. But in some cases employers browbeat or bully staff, making them insecure – and encouraging them to look for jobs elsewhere.

So? (Grade 8)

Employee retention is not only a factual measure, it also shows where faults lie within the business. If retention is especially low in one department, it should be investigated. There may be something as extreme as bullying or harassment going on – or it may simply be that the department boss is too quick to blame and too slow to give praise where it's due. Extra training could solve this problem.

Grade 9

Retention matters in all businesses. But in some it's absolutely crucial. High-tech companies such as Google hate to see staff leave – especially if they're going to a rival. Where skill levels are high, replacing an employee may be hugely expensive – yet still no match for keeping hold of the experienced worker. By contrast, retention may be low at KFC, but hiring and training a replacement is quite a quick and easy task. In an exam, think hard about the business in question.

Do remember that 100% retention may also be a problem for companies. Some 'new blood' with new ideas can be helpful. So the ideal retention rate may by something like 90 – 95% rather than 100%

Don't under-estimate the cost of replacing staff. For highly technical jobs the cost could easily run to £50,000+, given the cost of recruiting, training and the time it takes for new staff to **become**

Exam tip: exam papers often have business stories written by the businesses themselves. So they say a lot about being good to staff. Be willing to question this. Workers may have a different viewpoint.

Employee retention: 5-step logic chain (to get to top level of response)

Chain 1. When a manager leaves, so too does a lot of understanding of how the business works (1) … perhaps including strong relationships with customers (2) … based on years of working together (3)… that may have led to gaining regular, repeat business (4) … which may be lost if the customer decides to look elsewhere, or doesn't like the replacement (5).

Chain 2. When somebody leaves, the H.R. department must organise a replacement (1) … which involves finding a new shortlist of candidates followed by a careful selection process (2). Then comes a training programme that might take as long as the two years given to management trainees (3). This may be OK for wealthy firms (4) … but awkwardly expensive for smaller, less profitable businesses (5)

Training and Development

What? (Grade 5 basics)

There are many different ways of training and developing employees. When recruits join a company, they will get induction training to help them settle in. Then there may be regular weekly on-the-job sessions for all. Some shops open an hour later one day a week so that staff get regular training. Those same businesses may use off-the-job training when necessary, such as sending a new recruit to college one day a week to learn improved IT skills.

Staff are recruited based on their academic (GCSE/A Level/degree) or vocational (BTEC/CTEC) qualifications. Or in some cases they are recruited on to apprenticeship schemes which provide a combination of academic and vocational skills – all tailored to the particular industry.

Why? (Grade 6)

Staff like to feel comfortable in their knowledge – to be able to answer customer questions or solve their problems. So expertise matters – and training is the obvious way to provide it. Well-trained staff are more likely to be motivated in their job and far less likely to look around for a new job. So staff 'retention' increases; more staff stay in their job.

With technology developing rapidly, it's also vital to re-train staff to help keep on top of changes. In future staff may be working more with robots and 'intelligent' machines – and will need to learn how to do this. Retraining to use new technology will be an increasing part of working life.

How? (Grade 7)

Effective training starts with an understanding of what matters most to customers. If they want a fun, upbeat experience, then staff must be trained to provide exactly that. In other cases, the key may be intense training on new software systems – to ensure that customers' online ordering is quick, easy and accurate. In the best businesses, senior managers care about training, making sure that time and money is available for exciting but relevant activities.

So? (Grade 8)

With sports stars commentators often talk about 'natural' abilities. Read the diary of a sports star and it soon becomes clear that the 'natural' gifts emerged after hours and hours of training and practice. Great training makes people confident and helps their work and skills seem effortless. This makes it easy for them to make customers feel special.

Grade 9

Despite these positives, companies in the UK are among the meanest in Europe at paying for high quality training. It seems that they'd rather pay out higher dividends to shareholders than spend the company's money on their staff. If the business in the exam is one that does spend heavily on training, it deserves praise. And that business may have a huge long-term advantage over rivals that spend less on training. This is a great way to establish an edge over the competition.

Do remember the term 'induction'. It is the training you receive when you start working for an organisation. It helps the new employee feel welcome and comfortable – and therefore helps with motivation and retention.

Don't expect skill shortages to disappear any time soon, especially in the IT sector. If you have the right skills you will be in huge demand. UK companies talk a lot about training, but spend less on it than any other developed European economy.

Exam tip: in the Specification, the key phrases for exam questions are: 'development of the business' (as a result of staff training) and 'different training methods', which simply means on- and off-the-job training

Training & Development: 5-step logic chain (getting to the top response level)

Chain 1. A business with poor productivity needs to spend more on training (1) … partly to improve the technical skills of staff and therefore boost their efficiency (2) … and partly to make staff feel better looked after by the business, which can help with motivation (3). That, in turn, can help boost productivity (4) … due to better, trained technique plus better morale and therefore effort (5).

Chain 2. Many businesses provide plenty of training for middle and senior managers, but too little for shopfloor operational staff (1). This risks undermining motivation and retention among junior staff (2) … which in the long run damages the company's ability to develop and promote staff internally (3). So the business recruits managers from outside the business (4) … who may just stay for a year or two before leaving for a better-paid job elsewhere. (5).

Answering exams

Here are 3 questions where training and development are being tested. The main one is taken from OCR's specimen exam paper.

Q1. Explain one advantage to a business of providing ongoing training to its employees. (2)

Q2. A typical 9-mark question:

Analyse one way in which McDonald's could use each of these types of training for James*.

*James seems to be applying for his first ever job, armed with some recently-gained GCSE certificates

(i) Induction training (3 marks)

(ii) On the job training (3 marks)

(iii) Off-the-job training (3 marks)

Grade 9 Answers (questions on left)

Q1. Regular (ongoing) training sessions help build a higher level of understanding of what is wanted. In sport there's a term 'muscle memory' implying the muscles know what to do without being told. Ongoing training should do the same, e.g. knowing how to deal with a tricky situation without thinking about it.

Q2i) It seems likely that this job is James's first, so an effective induction programme will be especially important. He may not realise how tough most employers can be about lateness and absenteeism – and it would help him to be given clear information. He will also want to know how he can help speed up the process of getting fully trained, as that will boost his pay by 10% - and give him more confidence and knowledge when dealing with customers

ii) On the job training for James may start with a supervisor standing by his side as he learns to use the till accurately and speedily. The supervisor can make sure no mistakes occur that damage the profit margin. When he has mastered the till he can be allowed to get on with things – building up his confidence. Only then would it be sensible to try James on something else that's new to him.

iii) James may be hoping to develop more skills while at McDonalds, such as learning to be an expert at food hygiene. The company may pay for him to go on a one-day-a-week course at a nearby college. His eventual qualifications could help the local McDonalds fight food poisoning.

Why businesses train their workers

What? (Grade 5 basics)

Well-run companies see staff as an asset, to be improved all the time. They hope that staff will stay for years, perhaps even for their whole careers. Therefore they want staff to grow as the business grows, taking in new technology and new ways of working. But it must never be forgotten that training costs money and therefore companies want value for their money.

Why? (Grade 6)

If employees are trained to do a range of tasks, one absence is no problem. Another person slots into the role for a day or two. Production levels are unaffected and there are no delays in deliveries to customers. And well-trained staff have something else: the ability and confidence to try out new ways of working, perhaps finding ways to improve productivity. This makes the business more efficient and helps with staff motivation and retention. People like to be trusted and to show what they can do. Training helps achieve this.

How? (Grade 7)

Training is about more than knowledge of new systems or technologies. It can focus on developing team skills such as working together and problem-solving. Staff can be taken to outdoor courses where they work together to build a raft or a shelter for the night. This builds a bond between staff that helps them work better together, whether on customer service or on improving production quality.

So? (Grade 8)

When customers have a problem they want to talk to someone who understands and who has the authority to sort out a repair, replacement or refund – immediately. Well trained staff can do this, which helps hugely in boosting customer service and developing the reputation of the business. This helps build a reputation that takes brands such as Apple and Chanel to a level that makes customers willing – even enthusiastic – about paying high prices for the products.

Grade 9

At the top level in every sport, training is everything. A hugely successful golfer once said 'the more I train the luckier I get'. It's no different in business. If staff are really expert in what they do, it rubs off on customers and it helps in building a bond between the staff themselves. If staff say 'I work for Rolls Royce' with pride, the business is bound to benefit in terms of productivity, retention and sales.

> **Do** be clear on the link between training and customer service. And see its importance for a business. Most products sold today have similar levels of quality – so service levels can make the big difference

> **Don't** forget that training costs money – but don't overstate it either. Most UK companies spend less than £700 per person per year on training. That's probably far less than it should be.

> **Exam tip:** examiners are teachers, so of course they believe in education and training. So they'll usually respond well to a recommendation for a big increase in a company's spending on training.

Why businesses train staff: 5-step logic chain (to get the top level of response)

Chain 1. Training can transform performance (1) … as when David Beckham turned himself from a good to a great footballer (2). If a business wants to go from good to great, training is the way forward (3) … building bonds between staff and higher motivation (4) boosting production and productivity (5).

Chain 2. Anyone can buy a robot or clever machinery (1) … but research shows that differences in productivity are mainly to do with people (2). Staff need to be motivated and managers need to be trained (3) … so that they focus on building the confidence and competence of staff (4) … so that customers see the business as special (5).

Employment law

What? (Grade 5 basics)

Employment law affects the recruitment and employment of all staff. Important areas of the law include discrimination, employees' rights to a contract, holidays and hours of work. Businesses worry that legislation adds too much to their operating costs.

Why? (Grade 6)

For businesses operating within the European Union there is no problem, because all operate within the same laws. But UK businesses might be at a cost disadvantage compared with countries with weaker laws, such as America and less developed countries. British workers legally get 28 days' paid leave a year; in America the figure is zero. Does anyone in the UK really want to cut down on employees' holidays?

How? (Grade 7)

New laws affecting businesses set standards such as a minimum level of pay or a minimum standard for health and safety. In the UK 137 people died at work in 2016/17; in the equivalent figure for the USA was 5,190. Americans are eight times as likely to die at work than Brits.

So? (Grade 8)

Some politicians suggest that British business would be much better off without the 'burden of legislation'. In fact most businesses accept that current employment laws are a strong basis for operating today. Many businesses want to beat the minimum standards set by law – such as offering all staff a salary that's above the national living wage.

Grade 9

In countries with few laws governing business, workers can suffer. In China in 2008 nearly 100,000 workers were killed in workplace accidents. Since then China has passed tough employment laws. Of course, too may rules and regulations would stifle business enterprise, but there is little sign of that in the UK. The UK is regularly ranked in the top 10 countries in the world for the freedom for entrepreneurs to run their business competitively.

> **Do** remember that legislation brings benefits as well as costs. Many companies see the benefit from having a 'level playing field'

> **Don't** forget that UK businesses can – and do- have a big influence on UK laws affecting business. This is why there has not yet been legislation – as elsewhere – to force companies to have greater Boardroom equality by gender and race

> **Exam tip:** examiners like you to understand both sides to legislation. Yes it's good for employees to have protection, but sometimes it may be extra work (and cost) for businesses.

Employment law: 5-step logic chain (to get to the top level of response)

Chain 1. If legislation such as the minimum wage was set at too high a level (1) ... it might place such high costs on UK businesses (2) ... that it became difficult to make a profit when competing with goods from other, low-wage countries (3). That might force a UK business to close down in the UK (4) and perhaps open a factory overseas. (5)

Chain 2. Business leaders have always complained about new legislation (1) ... if they had been listened to there would still be children working in coal mines and up chimneys (2). More recently, businesses said the new minimum wage law would create waves of unemployment (3) ... but happily that proved incorrect (4). Today, no-one wants child labour – and few want to return to poverty wages. (5)

Production processes

What? (Grade 5 basics)

The purpose of business operations is to produce goods and services. That means managing the whole process from buying materials through production to customer delivery. There are three different types of production process: job, batch and flow. Most large businesses try to use flow production as often as possible. Small businesses use job or batch production.

Why? (Grade 6)

Flow production is used when a single product can be produced continuously on a conveyor belt production line – preferably 24/7. A good example would be Heinz Beans. The highly automated UK production lines produce 1.5 million tins a day. Little human labour is involved in the process, making the labour cost per tin very low, giving huge scope for high profits. Job production is used by small companies that tailor-make products to individual customer needs. In this case the labour cost will be high, so this can only work if the customer is willing to pay a high price – for a tailor-made wedding dress, for example. Batch production is a mixture of the other two.

How? (Grade 7)

To decide between job, batch and flow the business needs to consider the needs and wants of customers within the target market. Mercedes customers want a car tailored to their personal needs, so customers are offered thousands of options on each model. So flow production must be combined with job production (brilliantly, all done in an automated way on a largely robotic production line).

So? (Grade 8)

Production processes are rarely thought about by customers until something goes wrong. The wrong parcel turns up or the washing machine leaks. But many businesses build their reputation and brand name on their production excellence. And many more need to select the right production method (job, batch or flow) to help keep costs down and therefore keep prices competitive.

Grade 9

Large businesses like Apple want to make millions of identical phones cheaply. If they can sell them at high prices, that's a bonus. This provides an opportunity for small businesses to find niches the big companies aren't interested in. Then clever use of job or batch production makes it possible to provide exactly what the customer wants. Not every business can enjoy flow production.

> **Do** think about the difference between products and services. Both need to be run efficiently, but services are more likely to be tailored to a customer's needs, while products are more likely to be mass-produced, by batch or flow.

> **Don't** ignore batch production, which means producing a set number of an identical item, e.g. 24 pairs of size 10 green dresses. Batch production provides limited scope for automation.

> **Exam tip:** remember, flow = low labour costs, but inflexible production; job = high labour costs but flexibility; and batch production is somewhere in the middle: quite flexible but quite costly.

Production processes: 5-step logic chain (getting to the top response level)

Chain 1. Successful business operations need to combine good purchasing, the right production process and attention to quality (1) … all directed at what the customer wants or needs (2). When businesses get this right they are able to compete with the best, anywhere in the world (3) … and provide workers and managers with secure, perhaps well-paid jobs (4). So operations managers have a big and important responsibility (5).

Chain 2. Small businesses often start by batch-producing small quantities of a range of goods (1) ... perhaps finding independent shops willing to be brave with a new product range (2). But if Tesco decides to stock the products it may be necessary to cut the number of lines (3) ... and switch to flow production in order to produce high volumes at low costs (4). Then it should be possible to provide Tesco with the high profit margins they look for from any product they sell. (5).

Answering exams

OCR produces sample exam papers to help teachers. In these there is one question directly about job production. But there are many possible questions about improving efficiency or boosting profit where production processes are important

Here are 3 questions where business operations and production processes are being tested:

Q1. Explain how a business could benefit from more effective business operations. (3)

Q2.

Fender uses job production to manufacture its hand-made musical instruments.

Analyse the impact on Fender of using job production to produce these musical instruments. (6 marks)

Q3. Discuss the benefits to a business of using batch production. (6)

On the right are strong answers to these three questions. They are models for writing about the topic rather than models for how to score 6 marks.

Grade 9 Answers (see questions on the left)

Q1. It would be able to produce the right goods at the right time and get them delivered to the customer on time – all at a low enough cost to ensure that the business makes good profits.

Q2. If Bruno Mars wants a Fender guitar, it makes business sense to make a guitar that is so perfectly tailored that he wants to play it all the time. More play means more photos showing the brand name 'Fender' – and hopefully more sales. Job production can add value by tailoring to one individual, allowing a higher price to be charged. This, then, can benefit Fender further if they re-invest the extra profits into even better training to ensure even better guitars.

Q3. Batch production allows some benefits from automation while still keeping production quantities down to the level of demand. However cheap it would be to produce 2,000 XXL orange T-shirts, if the potential demand if for 40 – that's the number that should be produced. Low costs mean nothing if the products can't be sold.

But for some products it's important to restrict supply, producing only ten of one item and ten of another. Batch production has flexibility, whereas flow production is always the same.

Batch production allows businesses to match output to the wide range of different customer requirements, needs and wants.

Technology and Production

What? (Grade 5 basics)

Technology has a huge effect on production and efficiency. Productivity is a measure of efficiency. Not 'how much have we produced?' but 'how efficiently have we produced it?' Flow production allows huge volumes to be produced with relatively few workers involved – that's high productivity. And the main reason that flow production works is because of company investment in high-technology machinery, perhaps including robotics.

Why? (Grade 6)

Companies invest in modern, high-technology production because automation and robotics can provide all the things a business wants: high productivity, high quality and flexibility at a reasonable cost. If productivity rises, more can be produced for the same costs, allowing the business to choose between more competitive prices or rising profits.

How? (Grade 7)

To boost output in a job production system, 3D printing can be used. A 3D printer can be computer programmed to make every product made-to-measure to fit a particular need. In the past, job production meant human labour; today 3D printing is the high-tech answer. In flow production, as mentioned above, robotics may be important, but an automated conveyor belt system (invented over 120 years' ago) is also a key factor.

So? (Grade 8)

To build a successful business you need profit. This is the key source of capital to fund stable growth. So production efficiency isn't a luxury, it's a necessity. It is the way to boost efficiency, cut production costs and thereby allow the business to not only compete, but perhaps also start to beat the competition. If the company profit is invested wisely into updating automated machinery throughout the factory (plus extra training for staff) the profits should keep coming in future.

Grade 9

In the short term staff fear that greater investment in technology might mean fewer jobs. It would be silly to think that's never happened before. But despite waves of automation over recent decades there are more jobs today than ever before. So it's fair to expect that in the medium-long term there's probably no stopping the advance of technology – and little reason to fear that robots will be taking all the jobs in future.

> **Do** think about the benefits of technology. Twenty years' ago the paint on new cars was sprayed on by workers in constant danger of inhaling the spray. With robots it doesn't matter.

> **Don't** confuse 'productivity' with 'production'. Some people think that productivity is a posher was of saying production. It isn't; they're different. Production is output; productivity is efficiency.

> **Exam tip**: examiners are impressed by students who know that automated systems and robotic systems are not the same thing. Automation works best in a flow system, whereas robots are great for batch production as well.

Technology & Production: 5-step logic chain (to get the top level of response)

Chain 1. One way to boost productivity is to invest more on training (1) … which will help boost staff morale and motivation as well as effectiveness (2). If staff then work harder and smarter (3) … they will get more work done per day (4) … which boosts production and productivity (5).

Chain 2. Spending more on modern technology such as robots (1) … generates more output per worker (2) … and therefore boosts efficiency, as long as there is enough production to keep the robot working. (3). However with a small business a robot may only need to operate for a third of the day (4) … so the robot's purchase cost may not make financial sense (5).

Quality of Goods and Services

What? (Grade 5 basics)

Quality means different things to different people. For me, ice cream must be dairy; for you, it may have to be dairy-free. But we can both love ice cream. What links us, though, is that we want a good example of the ice cream we like. If the tub has been part-melted then refrozen in transit, we'll both find the texture disappointing, unpleasant even. So quality is to deliver the product the customer expects, i.e. to meet or beat expectations. To achieve this there are two main methods: quality control (Q.C.) and quality assurance (Q.A.).

Why? (Grade 6)

Why are there two methods for achieving quality? Largely because quality control is used by organisations that doubt their staff and therefore want to check everything before it's sent out. Quality assurance works by trusting staff to check their own work at every stage in the process, with the hope that no mistakes will get through to the end of the production line.

How? (Grade 7)

To organise a quality control system you need quality inspectors who understand the product well enough to spot imperfections. They operate at the end of the production line to stop poor quality slipping through to customers. But whereas you can look and see whether a car door fits well, it's harder to know if a car will stay reliable over the years. Quality assurance is better for dealing with what the inspectors cannot see.

So? (Grade 8)

Today, quality is taken for granted in most business settings. You expect your fries to be hot and crisp and your Coke to be cold. Businesses that fail to provide quality are likely to struggle. So quality is important not because it takes you to the front of the pack, but because it stops you falling behind. Quality supports the reputation of the business and helps to gain and retain customers.

Grade 9

If quality management is effective, no time will be wasted re-working poorly-fitting parts, and no money will be wasted when customers return a product (demanding their money back) or, worst of all, on product recalls. This allows businesses to control costs and therefore help in building a profitable, stable business.

> **Do** think about the importance of quality in the service sector. Hot food is wrecked if it's delivered cold, and a holiday ruined if the water in the pool is cloudy.

> **Don't** muddle Q.A. and Q.C. Most modern businesses try to build quality into every stage in the production process: so that's Q.A.

> **Exam tip:** the examiner has highlighted the link between high quality and cost control – and therefore profitability. That's a wonderful link for exam answers.

Managing quality: 5-step logic chain (to get to the top level of response)

Chain 1. If sales are slipping it's sensible to check how customers rate the product's quality (1) … and the service level that's supports the product (2). A switch from Q.C. to Q.A. may be called for, because quality assurance helps in building quality into every stage in production (3) … making it easier to cut wastage costs (4) … which can build a competitive advantage and help re-build sales (5).

Chain 2. If all the products in your market are produced to high quality standards you may need to boost your image by better design (1) … because there's more to quality than reliability (2). iPhone users love the quality feel that's been designed in (3) … which adds value (4) … enabling significantly higher prices to be charged (5)

The Sales Process

What? (Grade 5 basics)

Many products sell themselves, such as a Cornetto on a hot day. But others need selling face to face, either because of complexity or because the key consumer benefits are not obvious. For a product as complex as a modern smartphone, older customers especially need a lesson on how the phone works. And the car buyer may not realise there's a warranty guaranteeing free servicing for 3 years.

Why? (Grade 6)

The importance to businesses of providing good customer service comes, in the short-term, from the ability to turn a customer inquiry into a customer order; after all, that's the only thing that generates revenue. In the long term, good service is about getting first-time customers to become regular – and getting those same people to mention you to others ('word-of-mouth' or 'viral' benefits). A website says research exists showing that 68% of lost customers 'felt poorly treated'. So the sales process must focus on great customer service.

How? (Grade 7)

Face to face and telesales sales staff need terrific product knowledge, so they can answer every question and the personality to engage with customers. They also need the speed and efficiency to make sure that customers get exactly what they want, without delay. With e-commerce business, the key to selling is a well-designed website that is easy to navigate, allowing a purchase to be made with as few clicks as possible.

So? (Grade 8)

If customer service is vital, then training and motivating sales staff is equally so. It is easy to get this wrong. Huge bonuses for successful selling have encouraged bankers, travel agents and many others to push customers too hard – perhaps bullying elderly people to buy things they don't really want. Recently banks have had to pay out £billions in compensation to customers who have been 'missold' financial products. Well-run companies make sure that this could never happen. Poorly-run companies can't resist the temptation to make lots of money – now!

Grade 9

Customers love to be understood – to be pampered when they want it, but also to be dealt with quickly and efficiently when that's what's needed. The best sales person understands customer body language to see which approach is required. That hinges partly on the salesperson's intelligence, but can also be a lot to do with good training.

> **Do** think hard about the business situation. Sales and service are very different in a car showroom, a Lidl and for an online shop. Your exam answers must be adapted to the situation you face - just as in the real business world.

> **Don't** play down 'customer engagement'. This is the potential magic that takes good service (a smile, perhaps a handshake) into something special: real warmth, remembering your name, or giving a free sample - fresh from the oven.

> **Exam tip:** examiners want you to realise there has to be a balance. If great service adds too much to costs, then either prices must be increased or profits may be hit. But genuine smiles are free.

The Sales Process: 5-step logic chain (getting to the top response level)

Chain 1. For a new business like a café every customer is precious (1). The target is to turn as many as possible into regulars (2) … by a sales process that goes beyond efficient towards something special (3). Ideally, customers will then go out of their way to come to you (4) … providing a steady, stable income to help move the business beyond its break-even point (5).

Chain 2. With an online business the sales process is different (1) ... with a greater emphasis on simplicity and efficiency (2). Placing an order in two clicks would mean wonderful speed and efficiency of service (3) ... and the post-sales service must also be great – making it easy to send back unwanted items (4). Customer engagement is not important; speed, simplicity and efficiency take over (5).

Answering exams

OCR produces sample exam papers to help teachers. In these there is one question directly about customer service. But in OCR's marking guidance there are plenty of mentions of an effective sales process as a way of answering other questions.

Here are 3 questions where the sales process and customer service are being tested. The first is an OCR question:

Q1. Which one of the following businesses is most likely to use telesales?
A burger van
A petrol station
A school
An insurance company   (1)

Q2. A typical -mark question:
Analyse one benefit a business could gain from improving its sales process. (3)

Q3. Carter's coffee shop has just opened at the entrance to a busy commuter railway station. Ruby Carter is deciding whether to focus most on speed of service or most on product quality.
Justify which one of these options Ms Carter should choose.   (9)

On the right are strong answers to these three questions. They are models for writing about the topic rather than how to score maximum marks.

Grade 9 Answers (questions on left)

Q1. ANS: An insurance company

Q2. *An improved sales process can boost revenue by increasing speed and efficiency. A City centre ice cream shop doesn't make money in the winter; but on a hot day queues form quickly. The faster the service, the more people you can serve – and the higher the revenues. The boost to revenues should boost profits, allowing the business to invest more – perhaps in better staff training and therefore even better service in future.*

Q3. *In many locations this might be a difficult decision, but in this case speed of service is surely Number 1. Commuters won't return if getting a coffee makes them miss their train, so speed and efficiency is vital. It's also important for revenue, because customers will arrive at a similar time (before the train's due) so speed of service means getting more sales done in the window before the train arrives.*

On the other hand if the coffee's on time but undrinkable, all but a few addicts will melt away. So the quality must be acceptable. Quality certainly means the taste, but also means the cup (not burning the customers' hands) and the quality of service. A quick 'Good morning' and a smile takes up no time.

Overall, though, the speed of service is likely to be the key to high revenues at this location.

Customer service and engagement

What? (Grade 5 basics)

The heart of good customer service is understanding your customers and knowing your product. Some customers for a brand new BMW care what's under the bonnet; others care more about the entertainment system and seat positions. Top sales people quickly realise what the customer wants, and are as comfortable explaining the passenger features as they are with the technical stuff.

Why? (Grade 6)

The key is to achieve customer engagement. This means moving the customer from vague enquiries towards real interest – and perhaps a deal being done. Reasonable customer service (a smile; a polite question or answer) can lead to comfortable customers – but few sales. Great service leading to customer engagement can mean far more sales being achieved.

How? (Grade 7)

To turn your staff from being good with customers to being great is largely a matter of recruitment and training. Sales staff should be hired partly for their friendly, sociable, outgoing manner (as at Pret a Manger). And training should give staff the experience of what it's like to be a customer – to get a clearer sense of good service and poor service. The better the training the more likely it is that high sales figures will be matched by happy customers – keen to return in future, and perhaps even happy to spend a bit more next time.

So? (Grade 8)

The most important number is the percentage of customers who are retained. These are the ones who return in future. If this figure is high – say 80% - then not only will the company's sales figures stay high in future, it's also likely that these loyal customers will tell others. So it will trigger off rising sales. Also important is that if you can retain customers, those people will be less sensitive to the prices being charged. So it will be easier to put prices up in future. This helps with profit margins.

Grade 9

If product knowledge is an important step towards customer engagement, the cleverest companies build up that knowledge by giving sales staff regular usage of the product concerned. No-one knows an iPhone better than a regular iPhone user. So this can be an intelligent fringe benefit to offer staff. Give your iPhone sales staff a free iPhone contract – and give your BMW sales staff a week of free usage every few months. This will help with staff motivation as well as product knowledge (and therefore better customer engagement).

> **Do** think about the difference between customer service and customer engagement. Good analysis hinges on the often subtle differences between the meaning of different words

> **Don't** play down 'customer engagement'. This is the potential magic that takes good service (a smile, perhaps a handshake) into something special: real warmth, remembering your name, or giving a free sample - fresh from the oven.

> **Exam tip:** examiners want you to relate your answers, where possible, to the business objectives. If the company wants growth, then rising sales are all-important. If profit is the objective, higher prices may be more important

---

Customer service: 5-step logic chain (getting to the top response level)

Chain 1. In order to gain and retain more customers (and therefore boost sales) (1) … businesses want their sales staff to turn a good customer experience into a great one (2) … that holds customers' attention and engages them in the product (3). Ideally, this will turn an enquiry into a sale (4) … followed by further sales in future as the customer returns, perhaps many times over (5).

Consumer law

What? (Grade 5 basics)

Laws affecting business include those concerning consumer rights and safety. These ensure that UK consumers enjoy goods of a satisfactory quality. Businesses worry that legislation adds too much to their operating costs. But customers worldwide trust in the quality of UK goods, which helps in selling exports – and therefore provides UK jobs.

Why? (Grade 6)

If there were no laws to protect consumers, we might return to the old days when producers padded out bags of flour with powdered chalk – to cut the costs, while also cutting the quality of the bread. In China in 2008 six babies died and 54,000 ended up in hospital after suffering from contaminated baby milk. Although consumer laws are much tougher in China today, Chinese visitors to the UK still fill their suitcases with UK-made baby milk powder. Consumer laws matter.

How? (Grade 7)

To pass a new law means getting a majority of the votes in parliament. Some believe that today's consumers need more privacy protection from online giants such as Facebook and Google. But there is no certainty that parliament would provide a majority vote to support that.

So? (Grade 8)

Laws to protect consumers can be helpful to companies. They show a clear line between what's acceptable and what is not. When companies cross that line it can be hugely expensive. In one year the U.S. car giant General Motors spent more than $4 billion on 'product recalls'. Faulty production and quality management led to a colossal waste of money.

Grade 9

Many good companies work hard to offer customers great products at reasonable prices. They don't need to be controlled by consumer laws because they are acting responsibly in any case. But other businesses are so focused on making short-term profits that they cut corners, whether dumping waste by the roadside or producing 'vegan' foods with a bit of meat in. So consumer laws matter.

> **Do** take note of business complaints about the costs of meeting consumer laws. It may be that some laws add so much to costs that consumers end up paying higher prices

> **Don't** forget that some well-run companies like strong laws that prevent badly-run businesses from ruining everyone's reputation

> **Exam tip:** examiners tend to feel that consumer laws are a sign of a civilised country. New entrepreneurs may grumble, but the law helps steer them to produce good, safe products that customers want

---

Consumer laws: 5-step logic chain (to get to the top level of response)

Chain 1. If UK consumer laws were scrapped business costs would fall a little (1) … but the benefit to profit might soon be lost if, say, a food poisoning scandal made people eat more home-cooked food (2). Worse still might be a sharp drop in demand from abroad for UK-produced food (3) … which would cut our export income (4) and threaten many UK jobs. (5)

Chain 2. Even today there are problems with food fraud (1) … such as claiming that meat or milk is 'organic' when it isn't (2) … and therefore consumers shouldn't be paying the big price premium placed on truly organic produce (3). If there were no consumer laws, things would surely be even worse (4)… with companies finding it easy to deceive customers, just as – before food laws – the Bradford sweets poisoning case of 1858 was one of many crimes against consumers. (5)

Business Location

What? (Grade 5 basics)

In business, location can be a hugely important factor: think of the busy sweetshop near a station or the hamburger stall outside Wembley stadium. Important factors influencing location are nearness ('proximity') to the market, labour, materials and competitors. Now there's another huge influence: the internet in general and e-commerce in particular.

Why? (Grade 6)

Before the internet there were two main factors in location: direct convenience, as in having a coffee shop two doors from your work; and the alternative convenience from jumping in the car and driving to the nearest shopping centre, Now e-commerce threatens the second of these. As I'm writing this Toys R Us is closing down in the UK. Why go to a big self-service shed when you can buy on Amazon in a few clicks – and probably at a lower price?

How? (Grade 7)

To make a location decision a business must weigh up the potential revenues versus the costs at a range of possible locations. The rent on a shop in the main part of the high street might be 4 times higher than in a side street; but if there are 5 times more passers-by, it might be a price worth paying. If you're selling impulse-purchase goods such as Krispy Kreme doughnuts, it's wise to go for the high price/high passers-by site. If the products are a planned purchase such as a carpet, customers will find you when they need you – so stick to the side street.

So? (Grade 8)

Entrepreneurs with limited start-up capital are tempted to buy into a low-rental location. They think of the relatively low break-even position for the business and see it as the lower-risk decision. But you can't expect people to go out of their way for an impulse purchase. So a 'low-risk' option may be the riskiest of all.

Grade 9

Choosing the right location is a huge issue for a physical retailer, but unimportant to an online business. When you buy from ASOS you have no idea where the business is located (nor do you care). So ASOS can find a low-cost location where all that matters is getting the right staff and being close to good transport links. As the world moves more towards e-commerce, this pattern will increase – perhaps leading to falls in the rental values at shopping centres and in the high street.

> **Do** think about the circumstances of the business being looked at: e-commerce or physical; service or production; needing a high-skill workforce or a low-cost one?

> **Don't** ignore the costs involved in a good location. High revenues are no use if costs are even higher. Profit is the best way of judging one location v. another

> **Exam tip**: boost your marks by breaking location costs down into fixed and variable. Locating in Wales may mean low property (fixed) costs, but higher transport (variable) costs

---

Business location: 5-step logic chain (to get to the top level of response)

Chain 1. For a retail ice cream shop, physical location is critical (1) … because lots of ice creams are bought on impulse (2). So even though the rental cost may be high (3) … the higher customer numbers should more than pay for that (4) allowing the profits made in the summer to be high enough to get the business through the winter (5)

Chain 2. An ice cream factory can be located where there's the right mix of staffing and costs (1) … with refrigeration there's no need to be in a town centre, so costs can be kept down. (2) Fixed costs such as property and salary bills can push the break-even point too high (3) … so it's better to find a low-cost location (4)… and put more cost into higher-quality ingredients to make better ice cream (5)

Working with Suppliers

What? (Grade 5 basics)

Procurement means obtaining supplies. Businesses usually negotiate with a number of suppliers, then decide on the basis of quality and reliability, costs and credit terms. Some companies offer the business to just one supplier in order to get the best possible terms. A supplier with the chance of a huge contract may offer especially low prices.

Another factor is logistics: the organisation of transport and delivery of stock plus the final deliveries to customers. Efficient logistics help to keep costs down while ensuring the reputation of the business and a high level of customer satisfaction. If the supply chain is too long (perhaps from UK to China) it may be very hard to keep up with varying levels of demand from customers.

Why? (Grade 6)

In 2018 the huge aircraft-maker Airbus found problems with engines supplied by one of the top American engine-makers. Fortunately it had a deal with a second supplier. By switching to the second supplier, customer airlines could keep getting deliveries of their planes. Clever procurement saved Airbus from cancellations on its orders. With each A320 airplane priced at $101 million, this is no small matter.

How? (Grade 7)

Procurement starts by identifying the exact supply needs. Then setting up a shortlist of trustworthy suppliers. Then giving each supplier the precise order, asking each to quote a delivery price. That, plus assurances on continuing customer service will determine who wins the order. All these factors are part of the procurement decision.

So? (Grade 8)

Successful businesses such as Toyota or Jaguar build up long-term relationships with key suppliers. Instead of fighting over the cost of every deal, they work together on improving quality plus the speed and reliability of delivery. The important thing is to build up trust, so that the producer has faith in the supplier. For example, if the supplier is struggling to keep up with orders, it should inform the customer in plenty of time about the threat to the availability of the supplies.

Grade 9

With the rise in online e-commerce, procurement and logistics are becoming a central part of management. Millions may be spent on advertising, but if the customer gets the wrong product delivered, she won't return. The 2018 KFC disaster (outlets closures/chicken delivery problems) will not be forgotten quickly.

> **Do** remember that procurement can be done in one of two ways: switching suppliers regularly, to whichever is the cheaper; or building a relationship over time to work with a supplier on new innovations and ever-better quality

> **Don't** forget 'logistics' – the management of transport and delivery to keep costs down and customer satisfaction up.

> **Exam tip:** don't muddle logistics and procurement; examiners love to see business terms used in exactly the right way.

Working with suppliers: 5-step logic chain (to get to the top response level)

Chain 1. For a business with weak profits, costs can be cut by more careful procurement (1). There are advantages in having the same supplier for 20 years, but it's important to check, every few years, to see what else is on offer (2). Britain leaving the E.U. gives an opportunity to look again at possible UK-based suppliers (3) … who may be able to supply more cheaply thanks to lower transport costs (4) … allowing better procurement to help cut costs and re-build profits. (5)

Chain 2. For a fast-expanding business logistics can be a problem (1) .. because it's hard to get enough trucks, lorries and drivers (2) … to keep inward supplies and customer deliveries arriving on time (3). So it's important to hire a really capable Logistics Manager – and give her or him the power to make decisions such as buying new trucks (4) … without checking every decision with senior managers (5)

Role of the Finance Function

What? (Grade 5 basics)

Finance 'function' means the finance department – probably of a fairly big business. The purpose of the finance department is to provide two types of information for the company bosses: backwards-looking information about how much revenue and profit we made last month or in the last year. This is for the profit and loss account. And forwards-looking information to help in making decisions.

Why? (Grade 6)

Ultimately, all business decisions are about the future. If finance staff have done a cash flow forecast that shows a serious cash shortage between October and December, senior staff can decide whether to extend the overdraft or whether to push back a planned new product launch. To get planning decisions such as this right, senior managers need accurate financial information.

How? (Grade 7)

All figures that are about the future have every chance of proving wrong. A cash flow forecast requires a pretty accurate estimate of future sales, but that in turn will depend upon what rivals do and depend on overall levels of consumer spending. But companies (even schools) need to plan for how much can be spent – and when – so it's important to make the best possible estimates. Experienced staff can become quite good at this.

So? (Grade 8)

The finance function can have a big effect on business activity. In some companies it may have too big an effect. Overly-cautious finance staff may keep holding the business back from bold, innovative product launches or bold moves into fast developing countries such as Tanzania. In other cases, the finance function will be helping raise the capital to fund a company's growth plans.

Grade 9

Well-run businesses employ able people in their finance department and encourage them to develop accurate ways of forecasting cash flows and calculating break-even output levels. And make it clear that the finance function's job is to cooperate with achieving the overall business such as faster growth.

> **Do** remember that finance staff need to work closely with human resources and marketing staff to make sure that finance is available when needed

> **Don't** assume that every financial document is accurate. Break-even analysis is difficult to get right because costs don't split easily into fixed and variable – and cash flow forecasts can sometimes be little more than a guess into the future

> **Exam tip**: examiners tend to think that the finance function is the most important in the business, so any reference to 'checking this out with Finance' would add strength to many answers

---

Finance function: 5-step logic chain (to get to the top level of response)

Chain 1. Providing an accurate financial forecast can be expensive (1) ... as the data needs to be based on an accurate sales forecast (2) ... but it is likely to more than pay for itself by helping give accurate data (3) .... as that will form the basis for big business decisions such as whether the business needs to close some branches (4) or whether it can afford to launch a dynamic new product (5)

Chain 2. Finance may have a big influence on business decisions (1) ... because no-one wants to be so irresponsible as to ignore the financial consequences of a decision (2). This can stop companies being as brave as they might be over future plans (3) ... which could slow down the growth of the business and the economy more generally (4). In the best finance departments, staff see risky decisions as a natural part of business, not as something to be scared of. (5)

Reasons businesses need finance

What? (Grade 5 basics)

Businesses need finance for many reasons, such as when establishing a new business, running the business day-by-day, or funding expansion, including recruitment and marketing. Proud entrepreneurs don't want to lose ownership of their business, so selling shares or finding new partners are rarely popular. But few businesses like dealing with banks, so retained profit is by far the best way to finance growth and expansion. Clever businesspeople find the right source of finance to match the business need.

> **Do** think about the cost of the finance. The only 'free' finance is profit that's put back into the business (retained profit)

Why? (Grade 6)

Short-term needs should be matched by short-term finance. When buying stock from suppliers, nothing is better than trade credit. And if payments have to be made before customers pay their bills, an overdraft is a good way to finance needs that may be for just a day or two. The same logic applies to long-term finance. Long term needs such as buying robotic machinery should not be financed from short term sources. Retained profit or a 5-year bank loan would be far better.

> **Don't** follow the crazy logic of Dragon's Den, which makes it seem that obtaining finance is the clever/hard bit. Making a profit from trading – now *that's* hard.

How? (Grade 7)

Many of the sources of long-term finance come from outside the business and its founders. Crowdfunding, share issues or a new partner rely on persuading outsiders to risk their cash. This requires either a compelling social story (e.g. vegan, no-allergen, food) or a clear, convincing plan to make big profits.

So? (Grade 8)

Most entrepreneurs find that good ideas are easy to finance. Harder is to finance ideas with little distinctiveness. Would you invest in a new business that will be the 7th men's hairdresser on a high street? Probably not. So the key to getting finance for a new business is to find a real (preferably unique) business opportunity.

> **Exam tip**: avoid muddling bank loans with overdrafts. A bank loan is great for borrowing a single amount for several years; the flexibility of an overdraft makes it work for financing day-day business ups and downs.

Grade 9

When thinking of business finance, think of risk. The least risky sources are the owner's own capital and the company's own capital (its retained profits). The riskiest sources are: the cash flow strains caused by debt (loans and overdrafts) and the risk of losing control that comes from selling ownership – whether to ordinary shareholders or a new partner.

Clever entrepreneurs find a careful balance between these two risks.

Sources of finance: 5-step logic chain (to get to the top response level)

Chain 1. If you buy a lorry using your overdraft (1) … you'll face high interest charges over the years (2) … and by using up the overdraft you may struggle to get through tough times of year (3) … such as the lead-up to Christmas for producers of toys or tinsel (4). Shops expect deliveries in October but pay in January, so a big overdraft is needed to make up for the cash-flow shortfall. (5)

Chain 2. Crowdfunding works well for products customers are attracted to (1) … such as a new range of UK-produced, organic petfood (2). The customers' enthusiasm makes them happy to invest to help get the business going. (3) But many valuable business ideas don't sound that attractive, such as a cleaning service for work uniforms (4) … so crowd funding doesn't work in all circumstances. (5)

Suitable Finance

What? (Grade 5 basics)

When starting a new business, owners' capital is the most important. Many businesses start with no outside capital at all. And few banks want to take on the risks of a brand new start-up. Once the business is established, it's much easier to bring in capital from outside, especially if there's impressive growth.

Why? (Grade 6)

Growth sounds such a good thing that it's hard to realise that it usually requires the investment of lots of cash. If retail orders this year are double last year's, a manufacturer has to spend on factory expansion, more machinery, materials and staffing. The cash inflows come later. So finance for growth must be planned early, to get agreements in place with bankers or investors.

How? (Grade 7)

The first choice is between internal and external sources. Internal sources may provide enough capital, if the business is highly profitable, customers pay on time and there are some unwanted but valuable assets that can be sold. But that would be quite rare. Usually external sources are also needed – either loan capital or share capital. Selling shares is a safe source of capital, but does risk losing control of the business. Loan capital means monthly interest payments plus repaying that capital – both drains on cash flow.

So? (Grade 8)

The hugest business successes (think Amazon or Google) started by getting finance from bold investors. Later, they sold shares to private investors to bring in huge sums to finance continuing growth. Today they can finance their needs from retained profits. So different sources of finance are suitable at different stages in a company's life.

Grade 9

The questions of internal v external capital, plus share capital versus loan capital (debt) are very important. More important than either, though, is to plan early to know how much cash you'll need to get the business to the next level. And when you go early to the markets – to a crowdfunding site, perhaps – it's much easier for people to trust that you know what you're doing – and therefore invest in you.

> **Do** realise that because it's hard to establish a new business, crowdfunding investors should be cautious of risking too much capital. Many crowdfunded start-ups collapse – leaving investors red-faced.

> **Don't** forget that loan capital has an added level of uncertainty, because no-one knows what interest rates will be in a year or two's time

> **Exam tip:** when discussing sources of finance, the keys words are 'risk' and 'control'. Internal sources and also loan capital ensure you don't give away control – but perhaps at too high a level of risk

---

Finance for growth: 5-step logic chain (to get to the top level of response)

Chain 1. In business you pay today for cash inflows that come tomorrow (1) ... so growth needs to be financed with care – and cash (2). Most bosses start by looking at internal sources such as profits the business is making (3) ... but usually there's a need to look to external sources also (4) ... such as a careful balance between share and loan capital – to balance keeping control with the risk of debt. (5)

Chain 2. Growth is tricky to finance, but far worse is rapid growth (1) ... such as online fashion retailer Boo.hoo's 2018 growth rate of over 100% (2) The more rapid the growth the less likely that internal sources will provide much cash (3) ... because the speed of change is already such a financial drain (4). So rapid growth makes a flotation especially attractive – bringing in extra share capital (5)

> **Advice**
>
> The following section has worked examples (with answers) and calculations (with answers at the back of the book). These are hugely important for exam success, so please work through them with great care.

Business revenue and costs

What? (Grade 5 basics)

Revenue is the value of the sales made over a period of time, perhaps a month. It is calculated by multiplying Price x Quantity sold. So a chip shop selling 60 cod & chips at £6 each has made £360 of revenue.

Costs need to be broken down into two types: fixed and variable. Fixed costs are unaffected by the level of sales or output, e.g. rent and lighting. Variable costs vary as output varies, such as raw materials. The more crisps Walkers makes, the more potatoes they have to buy.

The formula for Total costs is: Fixed costs + (Variable cost per unit x Quantity). So if the chip shop uses £2 of fish and potatoes and has £150 per day of fixed costs, its total costs are: £150 + (£2 x 60 = £120) = £270 a day.

Do take care to read calculation questions twice over. They 'only' amount to 10% of the marks, but that gives scope for good students to gain 2 grades on others.

Why? (Grade 6)

Breaking costs into fixed and variable can help in setting prices. Restaurants typically calculate their variable costs on a dish and then multiply by 4 to get the selling price. A piece of steak costing £5 would be priced at £20 to the customer. That should leave enough to cover the fixed costs and still make an overall profit.

How? (Grade 7)

Costs are broken into variable or fixed depending on how they are paid out. One employee may be paid a salary (same every month); this is a fixed cost. Another may be paid per item produced (piecework) or sold (commission); this is a variable cost.

Don't muddle pence and pounds. If the examiner is using both, convert the pence to pounds and no mistakes can happen, e.g. 60p becomes £0.6.

So? (Grade 8)

Getting an accurate understanding of costs is important to a business, because it allows profits to be forecast: 'If we sell 3,000 of these, we'll make a £4,000 profit'. That, in turn, allows the business to plan how that £4,000 is to be spent, perhaps invested in improving the website.

Grade 9

The gap between revenue and costs can be widened if clever marketing or branding generates clear added value. The higher the added value the wider the gap – making it easier to generate high profits. Companies that show brilliance at added value, such as Apple and Chanel, often weave strong branding together with great design and great technology.

Exam tip: take real care over the term 'fixed costs'. Fixed does **not** mean 'don't change' it means 'don't change as output changes'.

Revenue and costs: 5-step logic chain (needed to get to the top response level)

Chain 1. To cut costs a business can tackle variable and/or fixed costs (1) Fixed costs can be cut by making administrative staff redundant (2) ... but that may lead to poor management and inefficiency (3) causing fixed and even variable costs to move up again (4) leaving total costs no lower than before (5).

Chain 2: To boost revenue a business must sell more items or manage to push the price up (1) without losing much sales volume (2). Selling more units is easy if consumer trends are with you (more gluten-free bread when consumers are focused on 'free-from' foods) (3) but hard when there's no growth in market size (4) perhaps forcing a business to revamp its packaging or find a new, better recipe for its product (5).

Worked examples (with answers)

Grade 5 question:

Q1. A company has weekly sales of 400 units at £12 each. Variable costs per unit are £3 and total fixed costs are £2,000 for the week.

Calculate a) Total revenue for the week and b) Total costs for the week.

ANSWER

1a) Total revenue = Price x Quantity

1a) Total revenue = £12 x 400 = £4,800

1a) Total costs = Fixed costs + Variable costs

Total costs = £2,000 + (£3 x 400) = £3,200

Grade 8/9 question:

Q2. An online fashion clothing site has monthly revenues of £12,000 from the sale of 240 items. It buys in the clothes for £10 per item and has total costs of £8,500.

Calculate:

2a) The fashion site's fixed costs per month

2b) The fashion site's average selling price per item.

ANSWER

2a) If total costs are £8,500 and total variable costs are £10 x 240 = £2,400, then fixed costs must be £8,500 - £2,400 = £6,100

2b) Total revenue divided by the number sold gives the average selling price.

So £12,000 / 240 items = £50 price per item

Business calculations (test yourself)

Grade 5 questions:

Q1. DF Ltd has monthly sales of 800 units, fixed costs of £1,500, variable costs of £2 per unit and a selling price of £8.

Calculate a) DF Ltd's monthly sales revenue and b) its total costs.

Q2. An airline sells 120 seats at £50 each and 80 at £90 each. The variable cost per passenger is £5 but the fixed costs per flight are £9,200.

Calculate a) the revenue per flight and b) the total costs per flight.

Grade 6/7 question:

Q3. A bakery sells 500 cakes a week at £2 each and 600 loaves of bread at £2.50 each. The bakery's total costs of £2,100 a week include variable costs of £1 per unit (cake or bread).

Calculate a) the weekly revenue and b) the weekly fixed costs.

Grade 8/9 question:

Q4. A surfing school charges £30 per one-hour lesson and pays its tutors £12. Last month the school's revenue was £15,000 and its total costs were £12,500 of which £5,000 were fixed.

Calculate a) The number of surfers taught last month (the sales volume) and b) The total variable costs per hour.

For answers see Section 8.2 (back of book)

Section 5.3: Revenue, Costs, Profit and Loss

Profit and Loss

What? (Grade 5 basics)

Profit is made when revenues are greater than costs. To calculate profit, use the formula: Profit = Revenue *minus* Total costs. If the costs are greater than the revenues the profit will be negative. That is known as a loss.

Profit is important for two reasons: it provides surplus capital that can be reinvested in the business to finance growth or to finance new equipment to help boost efficiency. In addition profit can be paid out to shareholders in the form of annual dividends.

For exercises to practise profit, see the right hand page.

> **Do** treat profit as a hugely important part of the long-term success of a business. Profits need to be high enough to finance the costs involved in keeping the business up to date

Why? (Grade 6)

Without profit few organisations would last long. Machinery and vehicles inevitably get older and more unreliable – so they need to be replaced. Profit can be used to pay for replacement costs such as this – enabling the business to stay up-to-date. Profit also provided finance for business expansion.

How? (Grade 7)

Profit stems from added value, in other words the ability to charge customers more than the cost of the materials used to make a product. The higher the gap between the selling price and the variable costs, the bigger the chance that fixed costs can be covered, leaving a surplus that is profit.

> **Don't** ever muddle revenue and profit. Oddly, students do it all the time. Revenue is just the money from sales. Profit is revenue minus costs.

So? (Grade 8)

If a business is making a loss, it is using more resources than it is creating in value to customers. So it acts as a drain on the economy. A profit-making business is not only making money for shareholders, it is also creating economic wealth for the community. Profit sometimes seems to be seen as a dirty word, implying that my profit is your loss. Generally, profit is an important and useful part of business.

Grade 9

Many exam questions revolve around boosting profits or overcoming losses. The logic is always the same: consider how best to boost revenues, taking care to think about the short-term and long-term issues. Then analyse how to cut costs without upsetting customers. Shrinking that chocolate bar seems a crazy way to do it, but finding a new, smaller, cheaper home for Head Office makes perfect sense.

> **Exam tip**: it helps you and the examiner if you start a profit calculation with a formula. Then follow it through (and the examiner can follow your logic)

Profit and Loss: 5-step logic chain (necessary to get to the top response level)

Chain 1. In the short-term cost-cutting is the surest way to boost profit (1) especially if you cut the things customers won't notice, such as staff job security (2) … perhaps by replacing full-time jobs with temporary jobs for lower-wage students (3). But if motivation is undermined within your workforce there may be a fall in productivity (4) making costs start to creep up again in the longer term (5).

Chain 2: If a business is making regular losses a solution must be found before the cash is drained from the bank accounts (1). One answer is to investigate which part of the business is making the losses (2) … and consider closing that down while refocusing efforts on the remaining business units (3). The remainder may actually be quite profitable (4) … or may benefit from greater management involvement to ensure better decision-making and the avoidance of costly mistakes (5).

Worked examples (with answers)

Grade 5/6 question:

Q1. A company has weekly sales of 500 units at £12 each. Variable costs per unit are £4 and total fixed costs are £3,200 for the week.

Calculate profit or loss for the week

ANSWER

1. Profit = Revenue – Total costs

Revenue = Price x Quantity

Revenue = £12 x 500 = £6,000

Total costs = Fixed costs + Variable costs

Total costs = £3,200 + (£4 x 500) = £5,200

So profit = £800

Grade 8/9 question:

Q2. An egg producer has monthly revenues of £72,000 from the sale of 72,000 boxes. Its variable costs are 50p per box and fixed costs are £20,000 a month.

Calculate:

2a) The producer's monthly profit

2b) The profit if a sharp increase in demand causes sales to double.

ANSWER

2a) Profit = Revenue – Total costs

If total variable costs are 50p x 72,000 = £36,000, and fixed costs are £20,000, then total costs are £56,000

So profit = £72,000 - £56,000 = £16,000

Business calculations (test yourself)

Grade 5/6 questions:

Q1. BGT Ltd has weekly sales of 100 units at £25 each. Variable costs per unit are £10 and fixed costs are £900 for the week.

1a) Calculate profit or loss for the week

1b) Calculate profit or loss if sales double

Q2. An online clothes store sells 400 shirts at £15 each and 250 scarves at £4. The shirts cost £4 each from Bangladesh and the scarves £2 each. The business has weekly fixed costs of £1,200.

Calculate the weekly profit.

Grade 6/7 question:

Q3. A farmer sells £10,000 of strawberries a day at £2 a kilo. The variable production costs are 40p a kilo and fixed costs are £6,500.

Calculate a) the weekly total costs and b) the weekly profit.

Grade 8/9 question:

Q4. A surfing school charges £30 per one-hour lesson and pays its tutors £10. Last month the school's revenue was £24,000 and its total costs were £15,000 of which £7,000 were fixed.

Calculate:

a) The number of surfers taught last month (the sales volume)

b) The profit last month.

c) The profit next month, if sales rise by 50%.

For answers see Section 8.2 (back of book)

Section 5.3: Revenue, Costs, Profit and Loss

Business Calculations (inc. Profit Ratios and ARR)

Percentages and Percentage change

A percentage is a hundredth, so 1% = one hundredth. If you need to find 20% of £8,400, multiply £8,400 by 20 hundredths, i.e. £8,400 × $\frac{20}{100}$ = £1,680.

To calculate percentage change, use the formula: $\frac{\text{Change}}{\text{Original}} \times 100$

So if sales have risen from £420,000 to £483,000, the % increase is:

$\frac{\text{Change}}{\text{Original}} \times 100 = \frac{£63,000}{£420,000} \times 100 = +15\%$

Please answer these calculation questions. Answers are in the answer chapter.

1. Last year UK sales of Nutella were £50 million out of a total market of £325 million for 'Spreads'. What percentage did Nutella have of the market?

2. A company has set a target this year to increase its use of recycled materials from 21 tonnes to 35.7 tonnes. Calculate the percentage increase.

3. Last year's profit was £64,000; this year's profit is £56,320. Calculate the percentage change.

Do really work on your calculations of % change. The chances of at least one question on this are about 99.5%. And you need this same skill in lots of other GCSE subjects as well.

Averages

A business deals with lots of customers and collects lots of data – often in the form of numbers. To make sense of them it can help to use averages. Instead of knowing the age of each of those who buy a product online it helps to know that the average age is 52. Even more, if you have another product where the average age of buyers is 29. Your approach to marketing is likely to be quite different with 29-year-olds than with 52-year-olds.

Some questions:

4. Here are the gross profit margins for all 4 products made by the AXZ Company: Product A 27.5%; Product B 48%; Product C 37.5%; Product D 53%. Calculate the company's average gross profit margin.

5. On average only 1 new product in 5 is a financial success. Does that mean that if a company has 4 flops in a row it will be successful next time?

Don't forget to show your workings when doing a calculation. But don't waste time writing down too much. The most important thing is the formula you're using. It helps the examiner but also helps you keep on track.

Gross and Net Profit Margin Ratios

A profit margin measures the profit as a percentage of the company's revenue. Gross profit is profit before deducting fixed overhead costs. Net profit is profit after the deduction of all operational costs including the cost of finance. The formulas are:

Gross profit margin = $\frac{\text{Gross profit}}{\text{Revenue}} \times 100$ Net profit margin = $\frac{\text{Net profit}}{\text{Revenue}} \times 100$

Q6. A business made £120,000 in gross profit last year from its £480,000 of revenue. Calculate its percentage gross profit margin.

Q7. This year the business expects to make a 30% gross margin on £600,000 of revenue. Calculate the expected gross profit total for the year.

Exam tip: A profit margin is no more complicated than a percentage. The key is to separate gross margins from net margins. Gross are the big ones, i.e. before deducting the fixed operating costs.

Section 5.3: Revenue, Costs, Profit and Loss

Average rate of return

This is a way to estimate the possible profitability of an investment. The Average rate of return (ARR) shows the estimated annual profit on an investment as a percentage of the sum invested. If the ARR is calculated at 8% per year while bank interest rates are 3%, the investment provides a potential bonus of 5% a year above the safety of leaving money earning 3% interest at the bank.

To calculate ARR, use the formula: $\dfrac{\text{Average annual profit}}{\text{Sum invested}} \times 100$

For example, if a £100,000 investment looks likely to make £42,000 profit over a 3-year period, the ARR would be:

£42,000 / 3 years = £14,000 annual average profit per year

ARR = £14,000 / £100,000 × 100 = 14% a year.

Calculations

8. A business estimates that a £40,000 investment will generate a total profit of £32,000 over the next 4 years. Calculate the ARR.

9. At a time when bank interest rates were 6%, ACG Ltd estimated it could make a £24,000 profit over 6 years from the investment of £80,000. Calculate the ARR on the investment and suggest whether or not ACG Ltd should go ahead.

Other Business Calculation Questions

10. FG Co. has weekly sales of £16,000 from a product priced at £4 which has variable costs per unit of £1.60. Weekly fixed costs are £7,200.

10a) Calculate the break-even point

10b) Calculate the margin of safety

10c) Calculate FG Co's weekly profit.

11. Calculate the answers for 11a – 11f from this cash flow forecast

All figures in £000s	January	February	March	April
Opening balance	80	b)	75	90
Monthly cash inflow	55	70	85	e)
Monthly cash outflow	65	65	d)	120
Net cash flow	a)	c)	15	(30)
Closing balance	70	75	90	f)

Answers:

Q1. £50m/£325m × 100 = 15.4%

Q2. Increase = 14.7 tons
% increase = 14.7/21 × 100 = 70%

Q3. Change = - £7,680
% change = -£7,680/ £64,000 × 100 = -12%

Q4. Average = all 4 figures added up (166) divided by 4 = 41.5%

Q5. No, there's probably still a 1 in 5 chance next time. Averages work over time, but no single result is predictable.

Answers (cont)

Q6. Gross margin was £120,000 / £480,000 × 100 = 25%

Q7. This year's gross profit is £600,000 × 30/100 = £180,000

Q8. The £32,000 total profit = £32,000/4 = £8,000 per year. So the ARR is £8,000/£40,000 × 100 = 20%

9. The £24,000 total profit = £24,000/6 = £4,000 per year. So the ARR is £4,000/£80,000 × 100 = 5%. Might as well leave the money in the bank and earn a risk-free 6% a year.

Answers (cont)

Q10a) Break-even point = £7,200/£2.40 = 3,000

Q10b) Sales are £16,000/£4 = 4,000, so margin of safety is 4,000 – 3,000 = 1,000

10c) Weekly profit = £16,000 – (£7,200 + £6,400) = £2,400

11a) (£10,000)
11b) £70,000
11c) £5,000
11d) £70,000
11e) £90,000
11f) £60,000

Break even

What? (Grade 5 basics)

The break-even level of output occurs when all costs are covered by revenues, leaving neither a profit nor a loss. There is a formula for calculating that point (see below) or it can be identified on a break-even chart. It's the level of output where the revenue line crosses the line for total costs. A break-even chart shows the level of profit at every possible level of output, from zero to the maximum production level.

Why? (Grade 6)

A break-even chart could help an entrepreneur decide whether to start a new business (is it realistic to get the sales volume needed to beat the break-even level of output?) and can help an existing manager make decisions such as whether or not to cut prices.

How? (Grade 7)

To calculate the break-even level of output:

Step 1: Calculate price *minus* variable costs per unit

Step 2: Divide fixed costs by the above total

e.g. If a business with fixed costs of £2,000 a week has a selling price of £40 a unit and variable costs of £15 a unit

Step 1: £40 - £15 = £25

Step 2: £2,000 / £25 = 800 units (the break-even level of output)

So? (Grade 8)

The real point of calculating break-even is to compare it with your actual sales level. The above example shows 800 as the weekly break-even level of output. That's fine if weekly sales are 2,000 units, as it means there's a healthy margin of safety. Sales can fall all the way from 2,000 units to 800 units before the business starts making losses. So the margin of safety is 1,200 units. But if sales are 900 units while the break-even level is 800, that's living on the edge.

Grade 9

Break-even gives an insight into the fundamentals of the business: is it profitable given the estimated future sales level? But it has a big weakness. It's only true at a point in time. It doesn't shows what's happening to sales (rising? Falling?) or trends in costs. Because it doesn't look ahead, it's not as useful as a cash flow forecast.

> **Do** remember how to measure profit on a break-even chart. It's the vertical distance between the revenue line and the total costs line

> **Don't** mistake the variable cost line for total costs. Remember that the variable cost line starts at £0 while total costs start where fixed costs start

> **Exam tip**: in the exam room, people often mix up break-even and the margin of safety. Remember, break-even is where the lines cross; and margin of safety is the gap between sales and break-even

---

Break even: 5-step logic chain (necessary to get to the top response level)

Chain 1. A break-even chart helps in making business decisions (1) because it shows the profit available at different levels of output (2) … perhaps helping a manager realise current sales are not enough, so new ideas are needed to boost demand (3). But if you rely too much on a break-even chart you might lose sight of cash flow (4) … which might be a big mistake, especially at the start of a business's life (5).

Chain 2: Calculating the break-even output is useful because it's more accurate than reading an answer off a graph (1) … which also allows a more accurate estimate of the margin of safety (2) … and therefore helps in evaluating how safe a position the business is in (3). A business wants its break-even point to be low (4) … and the margin of safety to be high (5).

Break-even chart for XY Motors

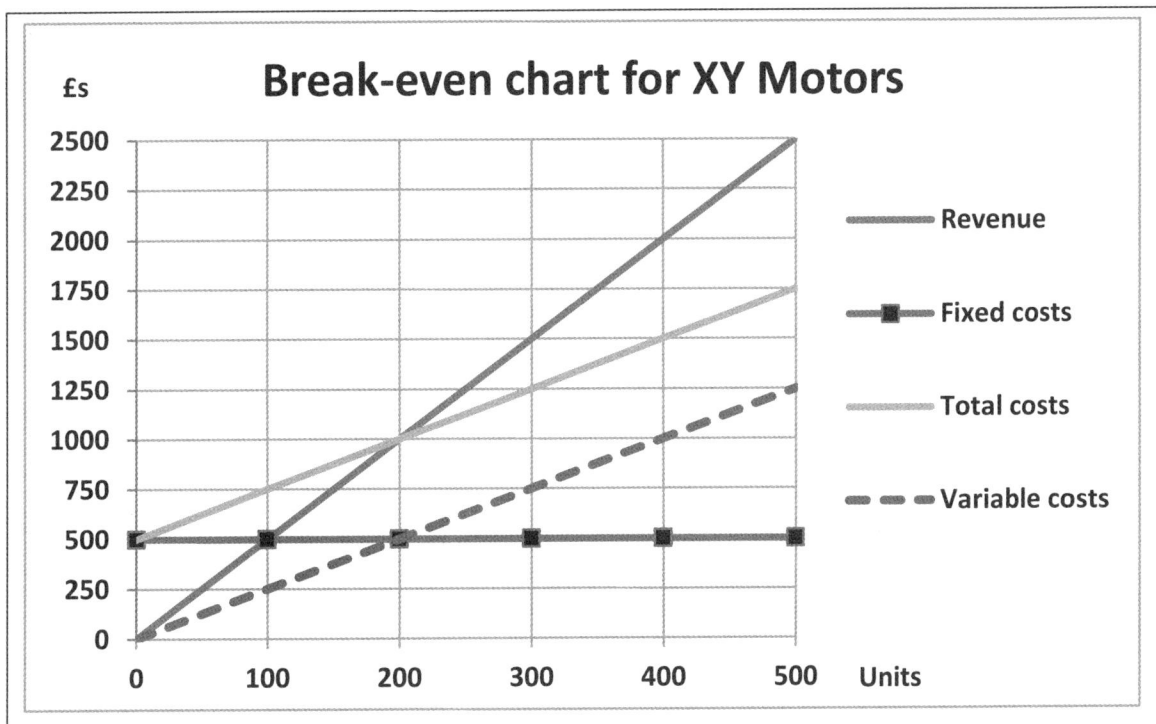

Look at the above break-even chart and answer the following questions (answers bottom right).

1. What profit does the business make if it sells all 500 units?

2. What is its margin of safety if it sells all 500 units?

3. Calculate the business's variable costs per unit.

4. Explain what happens if the business can only sell 100 units.

5. What might cause an increase in the fixed costs for the business?

Further Questions (answers to the right)	Business answers
Grade 5/6 question: Q6. Give two examples of factors that could cause variable costs to increase for a motor car manufacturer.	1. £2,500 - £1,750 = £750.
	2. 500 – 200 = 300 units
	3. At 100 units the total variable cost is £250, so the variable cost per unit is £2.50
	4. Total costs are £250 greater than total revenue, so it makes a loss of £250.
Grade 7/8 question: Q7. Identify two actions a business could take to reduce its break-even point.	5. Increase in rents; increase in interest rates
	6. An increase in supplier prices for components; an increase in raw material costs, e.g. the cost of sheet steel (steel to make the car's external panels)
Grade 8/9 question: Q8. Discuss the value of a break-even chart to a fast-growing business.	7. Cut fixed costs, e.g. move Head Office to a cheaper location; or push the price up
	8. Helps check profitability today, which may give confidence in future growth; but because the break-even chart looks at today only, it's not helpful for predicting the future.

Cash flow

What? (Grade 5 basics)

Cash flow measures the flows of cash in to – and out of – a firm's bank account. Cash inflows occur when customers pay up, when assets are sold off or when new capital is raised from outside lenders or investors. Cash outflows arise when suppliers are paid, when wages are paid and when loans are re-paid.

Net cash flow measures cash in minus cash out – perhaps over 24 hours or over a month. And when the cash out is greater than the cash in, 'negative cash flow' is occurring. Businesses often make a cash flow forecast to help anticipate when negative cash flows may cause a problem.

Why? (Grade 6)

Especially in the start-up phase, entrepreneurs are often told: 'cash is King'. Why? Because if you run out of cash – and can't pay suppliers or staff – the business will soon collapse. Your suppliers may even take you to court. So careful cash flow forecasting isn't an optional extra. It's always important, but especially in the cash-hungry times: start-up and whenever there's rapid growth.

How? (Grade 7)

Cash is tough when you start because suppliers don't know you well enough to give you credit. So you have to pay cash up front – whereas your business customers expect credit periods of perhaps 2 or 3 months. So your cash inflow is weak at the start, while cash outflows are big.

So? (Grade 8)

To cope with the cash flow problem at start-up (for almost every new business), there is only one solution: raise enough capital at the beginning to give a generous cash cushion. That cushion will be eaten away in the early weeks, but hopefully be big enough to cover the period until customer payments start arriving.

Grade 9

Many students understand cash flow problems at start-up, but are less clear about the strains caused by growth. When sales are booming, lots of cash is needed to buy more stock, hire and train more staff and perhaps build more factory capacity. Yes, the cash inflows will eventually arrive from higher customer sales, but the strain on short-term cash flow can be very tough. So look for rapid growth as well as start-up as occasions when you must warn of potential cash flow difficulties.

Do be practical about ways to improve cash flow. Few manufacturers can 'stop giving credit to customers' without causing customers to go elsewhere. Reduce credit periods, perhaps, but not cut completely

Don't ever muddle cash flow and profit. Your examiner cares about the (quite subtle) difference. Cash flow is about the immediate effect on the bank account; profit is more long-term

Exam tip: build your analysis of 3+ mark questions by breaking cash flow into cash inflow and cash outflow. Then show why inflows may be slowing and why outflows may be rising

---

Cash flow: 5-step logic chain (necessary to get to the top response level)

Chain 1. If monthly net cash flows are negative (1) the cash you started the month with will be lower at the month-end (2) ... and may even drag the bank account 'into the red' (3). This can only happen if the business has already agreed an overdraft with its bank (4) ... without an overdraft the bank will refuse to make any more payments – causing a serious cash flow crisis (5).

Chain 2. A boom in customer orders seems a reason to celebrate ... but the impact on cash can be tricky (1). You have to pay out more cash to suppliers, on staff overtime and perhaps to buy faster machinery (2) ... but the extra inflows from sales will take a few months to arrive (3). Until then, the business may operate with negative cash flow (4) ... causing the bank to lose confidence in you. (5)

Worked examples (with answers)

Grade 5/6 question:

Q1. A company's cash inflow this month is £7,000 and its outflow is £7,500. Its start-of-month opening balance was £3,000.

Calculate its end-of-month closing balance.

ANSWER

1. Month-end closing balance is:

Opening balance + monthly net cash flow

So £3,000 + (£500) = £2,500

Q2. Grade 6/7 question:

Calculate the answers to each of the missing numbers a) to e) in the table below.

	Jan	Feb	Mar
Opening balance	£1,200	£700	d)
Monthly cash in	£400	£800	e)
Monthly cash out	a)	£700	£900
Net cash flow	(£500)	b)	£200
Closing balance	£700	c)	£1,000

ANSWERS

2a) £900

2b) £100

2c) £800

2d) £800

2e) £1,100

Business calculations (test yourself)

Grade 5/6 questions:

Q1. BVK Ltd has cash outflow this month of £30,000 and a cash inflow of £33,000. Its end-of-month closing balance will be £10,000.

Calculate its start-of-month opening balance.

Grade 7 question

Q2a) A clothing business has an unexpected boom in orders in July, thanks to a celeb tweet that goes viral. Calculate the missing items within its cash flow.

	June	July	August
Opening balance	£3,000	£3,300	(£900)
Monthly cash in	£2,500	£2,800	£3,900
Monthly cash out	£2,200	c)	£6,900
Net cash flow	a)	(£4,200)	d)
Closing balance	b)	(£900)	e)

Q2b) Briefly explain how it is possible for a business to have a negative end-of-month closing balance. (3)

Grade 8/9 question:

Q3. Discuss why the cash flow forecast for a new pizza delivery business might prove to be incorrect. (6)

For answers see Section 8.2 (back of book)

Ethics, the Environment and Business

What? (Grade 5 basics)

Ethical considerations affect a wide range of business decisions. The boss may know that the mainly-female accounts department is underpaid compared with mainly-male dispatch workers – but do nothing – hoping no-one notices. The boss may also know that the sales team's triumph in South America probably involved bribery – but do nothing. Both examples raise big ethical questions.

The environment also relies on morally sound business decisions. In the past, many businesses have polluted rivers or damaged forests. Companies today are clearer that they are likely to get caught – and blamed. So they take more care over waste disposal, pollution and sustainability – and therefore climate change.

Why? (Grade 6)

Ethics and environment matter to shareholders when a company develops a poor reputation. After a huge oil spill in the Gulf of Mexico, BP sold off most of its U.S. operations – because U.S. customers would no longer deal with BP. In a world of social media viral storms, no business should make itself vulnerable to attack.

How? (Grade 7)

From the first day, new staff should be told that the business cares about doing the right thing – and about its reputation. Staff should know that if they have a slight doubt about the ethics of a situation – they should ask their boss. And from the Directors there should be consistent evidence that ethics matter.

So? (Grade 8)

The most obvious ethical questions arise in ethics versus profit. If we cut out 25% of the sugar in our Coco Pops, will sales fall? Yes, but we think it's the right thing to do. Naturally, decisions such as that are very rare. Most companies hope to keep ethics 'quiet', while getting on with making money as usual.

Grade 9

The biggest test of a company's ethics is what it does when no-one's looking. Good companies get on with doing the right thing, even though no-one can see. Long ago, Marks & Spencer was like that: paying staff well and paying suppliers early. Companies that boast of their high standards deserve careful questioning.

> **Do** be willing to show the examiner that you care about ethics and/or the environment. It's fine to say that a company might make more profit doing one thing, but you think it's ethically proper to do something else.

> **Don't** hold back from criticising unethical companies, but remember that companies under financial pressure may cut corners to stay alive – not ideal, but perhaps forgivable

> **Exam tip:** when thinking of the environment, always think short-term (today's bad smells) versus long-term (global warming and sustainability). Poorly run businesses cover up the smells and don't deal with the long-term problems

---

Ethics & the Environment: 5-step logic chain (getting to the top response level)

Chain 1. A well-run business acts responsibly towards suppliers, customers, staff and pensioners (1) ... which is easy to do if the company's profits are high enough (2). Therefore it's correct for the boss to focus on making the right decisions to generate high profits (3) ... relying on other staff to make the right ethical decisions about the stakeholders (4) ... especially to look after the weakest (5).

Chain 2. Some small businesses only think about short-term profit (1) ... such as the builder who illegally dumps waste by the roadside instead of paying for proper waste disposal (2). This is why laws exist to regulate business actions relating to the environment (3). The pressure to cut corners always exists in business (4) ... making laws & regulations a helpful way to set out what's right and wrong. (5)

Answering exams

Exam questions on ethics or the environment are naturals for 6, 9 and 12-markers. Both topics are quite easy to develop into fuller answers.

Here are 3 questions featuring ethics and the environment:

Q1. Define the term 'ethics'. (1 mark)

Q2. Discuss the benefits to a business of taking care over the environment. (6)

Q3. Grayson's Ltd produces gluten-free doughnuts which are sold in all outlets of two large UK supermarket chains.

In order to improve its prospects for long-term growth, Graysons has two options:

Option 1. Higher ethical standards

Option 2. Higher profits.

Justify which one of these options Grayson's should choose. (9)

On the right are strong answers to these three questions. They are models for writing about ethics and the environment rather than models for how to score 6 or 9 marks.

Grade 9 Answers (Qs. on the left)

1. Moral standards in business.

2. A key environmental problem is finite resources. In other words the planet must eventually run out of materials such as copper. A business can help the environment by a 'lean' approach, minimising resource usage and wastage. This also means minimising business costs, therefore helping to build up profits.

A second benefit can come from repeat business due to customer loyalty. If customers see that a product if '100% recyclable' and boasts 'Two new trees planted for each one used' they may be willing to pay a little extra. Higher sales volume plus higher prices add up to a significant boost to revenue and profits.

Q3. To work to higher ethical standards could help the business be more attractive to stakeholders. Customers might be thrilled if the gluten-free dough was 100% organic, implying less stress on the environment. Indeed customers might be willing to pay a price premium – enough, perhaps, to cover the higher cost of ingredients. Staff would also be pleased partly because of the reassurance that their job has value, but also because of happier customers. The adoption of '100% organic' is not only ethically worthwhile, it adds sufficient value to pay for itself.

On the other hand focusing on ethics might be self-defeating. Gluten-free or not, a doughnut can never be the subject of much ethical respect. It's just yummy calories. If organic adds to the selling price demand may fall back to a small niche – making it hard to make a profit. There's nothing ethically impressive about business failure.

The Economic Climate

What? (Grade 5 basics)

The economic climate affects businesses in many ways, largely through changes in:

- the levels of consumer income known as the economic cycle
- changes in the number of jobs and therefore unemployment
- government policy towards the economy, e.g. a cut in taxes

Why? (Grade 6)

Changes in the economy can have serious effects on businesses when they are unexpected. A business spending big on a new, bigger factory may suddenly be hit by a 'recession'. Falls in consumer incomes throughout the economy lead to falling sales. So the company spending on growth is hit by falling revenues. Lower revenues and rising costs can squeeze profits dramatically.

How? (Grade 7)

The UK economy is affected sharply by what's happening in linked economies in Europe and America. If they are weak we sell fewer goods to them, so our businesses suffer. And if our government wants to follow 'austerity' policies such as cutting its spending on disability benefits – that cuts total consumer spending and therefore cuts business revenue.

So? (Grade 8)

Business bosses want to be in control. They like to establish their own objectives then plans to meet or beat them. Unexpected economic changes can get in the way. A weak economy may force firms to cut back on jobs. The newly unemployed cut their spending. This hits company revenues – possibly forcing even more job cuts.

Grade 9

Businesses always try to influence the things they can't control. They try to persuade politicians of the economic policies that are 'right' for business and the economy: perhaps keeping interest rates low in order to keep consumer spending high. And they may push for cuts in unemployment pay, to force those without jobs to hunt for work. Sometimes the policies being pushed for are good for businesses and their shareholders, but less good for employees and less good for the long-term health of the UK economy.

> **Do** be clear that economic change can overwhelm businesses. A sudden recession can catch businesses out. Businesses want stability, not drama

> **Don't** forget people. The exam questions are about businesses, but the answers are richer if you think about the impact upon people. Beware of seeming keen to see real people sacked.

> **Exam tip**: examiners love you to know that businesses are affected differently by economic factors. Sales of toilet paper or ketchup are little affected by economic ups and downs. But sales of sports cars and other luxuries can be affected hugely

---

Economy and Business: 5-step logic chain (getting to the top response level)

Chain 1. When a recession hits, consumer spending falls in response to worsening consumer (1) and business confidence (2) causing consumers to be more cautious about spending (they'd rather save 'for a rainy day') (3) and businesses to cut back spending on new investments (4) creating a risk of job losses… and a further downturn in consumer spending (5).

Chain 2. If economic growth in Europe and America boosts our exports (1) … and therefore UK business revenues (2) … consumer and business confidence rises, providing more jobs and cutting unemployment. (3) If companies respond by increasing their spending on investment (4) the whole economy benefits, including more tax revenue flowing into the government's bank account. (5)

Globalisation

What? (Grade 5 basics)

Globalisation is the increase in world trade that has brought the world's economies closer together. American imports such as Starbucks and iPhones are to be found in almost every country. And the UK has global exports such as whisky, Burberry coats and Ted Baker clothes. Some businesses such as HSBC bank may change the location of their Headquarters; HSBC moved from Hong Kong to London to help it become a global bank.

Why? (Grade 6)

The urge to operate globally comes from the huge opportunities in booming economies such as China. Between 2007 and 2017 car sales in the UK rose by 4%; in China they rose by 306%. Companies such as Jaguar Land Rover have to get into the Chinese market to have any long-term prospects. As well as China, India, Vietnam, Thailand and Indonesia are also growing rapidly.

How? (Grade 7)

Multinational companies such as Shell become global by opening oil refineries and petrol stations in many countries across the globe. Others achieve the same goal by keeping their roots firmly in the UK, but growing globally by exporting widely from the UK. ASOS – the online fashion retailer – has grown remarkably by showing a good understanding of young people worldwide.

So? (Grade 8)

During the period of rapid growth in world trade (1980-2008), extreme poverty in the world fell by 750 million, so globalisation proved helpful for the world's poorest. So American President Trump's attack on trade in 2018 seemed odd. He imposed big tariffs (taxes on imports) on fridges, solar panels and steel – hitting goods from China and South Korea especially. Although he justified his actions by saying "America First", the impact would have been to hit jobs and incomes in Asia (and to increase the price of fridges for American households).

Grade 9

Globalisation brings benefits to rich and poor countries alike. But there are also downsides. Some people hate to see a Starbucks and a McDonalds in every town in the world, as they'd like to see local, independent businesses thrive. And many worry that some multinationals are so rich and powerful that it's hard for governments to control them – and very hard to get them to pay their taxes. Overall, though, workers and consumers in poor countries welcome the arrival of a multinational that plans to locate a factory or open shops nearby.

Do think about the value to workers in poor countries of the chance of a job with a big multinational company – good training, good salary and better career prospects

Don't doubt that some multinationals damage globalisation by their lazy approach to poorer countries' environment. Both Shell and BP have a poor record – especially in Nigeria and the US

Exam tip: ASOS and Ted Baker have shown the power of UK fashion business in internet/e-commerce sales worldwide. Even smallish UK business may have the chance to compete internationally by clever use of e-commerce

---

Business and globalisation: 5-step logic chain (to get to top level of response)

Chain 1. Every UK business should look for global market opportunities (1) … because countries such as China and India are growing faster than ours (2). A fully globalised business might try to produce new products designed for new markets, such as China (3) … or open a factory in China, as Jaguar Land Rover has done (4). The key is to design products that are wanted (nearly) everywhere (5)

Chain 2. A UK company may decide to build sales in Asia or Africa by designing products for these markets (1) … making it hard for competitors to keep up (2) … unless they invest heavily in new products (3). In the past Marks & Spencer has struggled to sell profitably overseas. (4) … perhaps because they wanted to sell UK items abroad instead of designing ones especially for local markets (5)

How businesses compete internationally

What? (Grade 5 basics)

For most businesses, competition is a constant threat. Currently it's extremely tough for toy and clothes shops because of the rise of internet retailers such as ASOS. In the high street competition is tough for restaurants because there are so many rivals – often right next door. But things get even harder for businesses such as Jaguar Land Rover (JLR) who have to take on motor giants such as VW, Toyota, Mercedes and so on. JLR has to compete internationally.

Why? (Grade 6)

Years ago manufacturers could succeed by selling goods in their own local area or region. But it's easy for foreign firms to export to the UK, so companies such as the German Mercedes or BMW can easily sell their products in the UK. For a British car company to survive, it needs to find markets overseas to make up for the lost sales in the UK.

How? (Grade 7)

How can businesses make sure they survive fierce international competition? Of course they can't 'make sure'. But they can work harder to give customers what they want – in lower prices and better product design and quality. When competition is tough it's time to give customers better value and – especially – more smiles and more efficient service. Online goods must be delivered on time, as must UK goods exported to Germany or America. Customers always matter – but just that bit more when competition is strong.

So? (Grade 8)

In the exam, show that you recognise how tough competition can be for the management of a business – and perhaps tougher still for staff. But as customers, we love a bargain price, we may even love a Closing Down Sale. International competition pitches customer satisfaction against worker security.

Grade 9

For companies, more competitors means more pressure to keep costs down – which can be tough on staff, who may be pressed into signing job contracts that give them few rights – to pensions, say, or sick pay. But for consumers competition means lots of special offers and fewer price rises. In effect, consumers get better value for money while employees find things a lot tougher.

> **Do** be clear that globalisation gives huge opportunities to companies, to help them grow huge. But fiercer competition creates losers as well as winners.

> **Don't** doubt the logic of the business world. If a poorly run business is closed down by the success of a brilliant newcomer, customers are better off.

> **Exam tip:** international competition is increasing achieved through international branding, with companies such as Apple, Nike, Chanel and Nintendo succeeding worldwide.

International Competition: 5-step logic chain (to get to the top response level)

Chain 1. If a business faces fierce competition it may need a tight focus on keeping costs down (1) … especially costs that don't affect customers such as the location of Head Office (2) … but it's also vital to work on details customers care about, such as on-time deliveries (3) … which may increase operational costs (4). Getting this balance right is essential for the business to survive and thrive. (5)

Chain 2. Some businesses have an easy life because they face little competition (1) … such as Wrigley (95% of the UK market for gum) or Virgin Rail London-Manchester (100% share, i.e. no direct competition) (2). This usually leads to greedy pricing (3) … and few new ideas on improving customer service (4) which shows that competition is valuable for customers (5)

Interdependence of the four business functions

What? (Grade 5 basics)

Interdependence of the business functions means the way they link together and depend on each other. So the operations, finance, marketing and human resource departments must work together to achieve the company's objectives. They must plan the future together but also work together day-by-day to meet or beat customer expectations.

Why? (Grade 6)

The reasons why the functions are interdependent are obvious in a restaurant. As customers arrive they must be welcomed, seated and given a menu. The style and look of the menu will have been handled by the marketing expert, who may also have decided on the prices. The menu will set up expectations that the food and service will have to live up to. High prices but just-OK food in small portions – and the game is over. Or if the service operation is poor, so the food arrives cold – game over. Marketing, operations and human resources must work together.

How? (Grade 7)

The way the Japanese handle this is to use horizontal 'promotions'. In other words being moved over from marketing to operations is regarded as a promotion, because it shows the business is thinking about the employee's career development. A lesser worker would stay in the same marketing job for ever. In this system, by the time staff become managers they know the different functions – and are familiar with the staff in each, making it easier to work together.

So? (Grade 8)

It's quite easy to run a single department (function) such as marketing; much harder to run a whole business. The business only succeeds if all the staff are working towards the same objective. If the head of marketing wants a price cut on a leading brand, it must be discussed weeks ahead with operations (who'll need extra supplies) and human resources – to organise overtime for the staff.

Grade 9

The more the functions work together the more successful the business will be. If the bosses don't want to use horizontal promotion they must find another way to bring their people together. In a small-ish business Friday-night drinks (bought by the boss) will help. In a larger company it may be necessary to organise something involving all staff – perhaps a big training programme or a sports tournament.

> **Do** focus mainly on the finance function; see it as the core around which the other functions move – because that's how your examiners see it.

> **Don't** doubt that in some businesses the four functions work poorly together. They may see themselves in competition for the boss's favours. They may prefer to 'beat' their rivals than work with them.

> **Exam tip:** just as examiners like you to see that the four elements of the marketing mix should work together, the same is true here. The four departments of the business must work interdependently for success to be achieved.

Interdependence and decisions: 5-step logic chain (for top level response)

Chain 1. When faced with a business problem good companies get people to work together (1) … especially for marketing to work with operations and human resources (2). Working together helps prevent serious mistakes being made (3) … and helps in coming up with new product development ideas (4) … that may enable the company to build up its revenue and its profit margins (5).

Chain 2. For a successful business such as Apple, the only risk is of complacency (1) … especially among middle and junior staff (2). Working together, the staff within the 4 functions can identify things that might be going wrong (3) … and work together to solve them (4). This may help stop gaps emerging that competitors could move in to. (5)

Interdependence and decision making

What? (Grade 5 basics)

Businesses should be ambitious, but also realistic. Marketing managers may want to run a Buy One Get One Free (BOGOF) but the operations (factory) staff may not be able to produce the extra stock needed. So the decision must be to scrap – or postpone this decision. When the four functions work together they can reduce the number of mistakes – and therefore help improve the company's decision-making.

Why? (Grade 6)

The four functions are interdependent, so they rely on each other. One department cannot act without talking to the other three. When they work together the business is much more likely to succeed with: crowd-pleasing new products; keeping up with sales going crazy before Christmas; and the crucial thing of keeping existing customers happy.

How? (Grade 7)

If the boss of the company understands the four functions well, it will be tempting to take decisions – then tell them what to do. But it would be better to meet together to discuss opportunities – and possible problems. No-one will understand marketing decisions better than the marketing staff – and so-on through the four functions.

So? (Grade 8)

Today markets change rapidly as fashions and technology keep changing. So it's great to be the first with a new type of phone or affordable fashion straight from the catwalk. Speed matters. Quick, effective decision-making relies on the four functions working together. When marketing, finance, operations and human resources believe in their interdependence they'll work together to help the business succeed.

Grade 9

All business decisions are about the future. Therefore they are uncertain because no-one knows what the future will be. So no business can get all its decisions right. Success comes from being wrong less often than others. And this will be easier if the four business functions work together.

> **Do** see that right decisions may not prove that the boss is brilliant. It may be the boss is helped by brilliant staff – working together in the four functions.

> **Don't** be too harsh on businesses (or bosses) who've made a wrong decision. The key is how well they recover from it.

> **Exam tip**: there are always two sides to every difficult decision. Reflect that in your answers to 9+-mark questions. Then draw your conclusion about which side is the stronger.

Interdependence and decisions: 5-step logic chain (for top level response)

Chain 1. The toughest decisions are the ones no-one saw coming (1) … like having to close the factory for a month because sales are so weak (2). Marketing staff may be the first to hear of problems from customers (3) … and can help the business by quickly telling operations and human resources about the threat to sales (4) … allowing a speedy decision on 'mothballing' the factory. (5)

Chain 2. Decisions are also about opportunity and potential success (1) … which is helped enormously by staff talking to each other (2). With a new product, the business ideal is something that's easy to make but brilliant for the customer to own (3) … which needs a lot of work between the marketing and operations functions (4). These two departments then need support from finance and human resources to ensure overall success. (5)

Impact of risk and reward on business activity

What? (Grade 5 basics)

This section of the course focuses on business decision making. So business activity means the day-to-day and longer-term issues that have to be decided upon. Risk and reward feature strongly in marking out the difference between some businesses and others. Big, successful businesses such as Cadbury want to avoid mistakes and therefore risks. When you are the biggest force in the UK market for chocolate, you know that rewards will keep coming as long as you don't take risks that could backfire.

Why? (Grade 6)

For new, young businesses, it can be worth taking risks to try to break in to markets. Unless they take risks they cannot achieve high rewards (such as big profits and big dividends paid out to the owners). When these businesses mature they may take fewer risks because they have a lot of profitable sales to protect. When Google started it was a brilliant risk-taker; today it's hugely wealthy and much more cautious.

How? (Grade 7)

Risk-taking affects business activity constantly. A growing coffee chain may have to decide whether to spend £500,000 on a property in a great position by the train station – or £125,000 on a similar-sized property further down the high street. One manager may refuse to risk £500,000, and later find that the £125,000 site struggles to break even. In business, it's usually the case that the higher the risk the higher the potential reward.

So? (Grade 8)

The ideal business leader enjoys taking bold decisions that involve risk – but only when the rewards are high enough to justify those risks. Some bosses are so keen to 'prove' themselves that they take unnecessary risks – and may get fired. But equally unsatisfactory is a timid boss who keeps putting off decisions – scared of the risk of failure.

Grade 9

Different stakeholders have different attitudes to risk and reward. The last thing staff want is the risk of a mistake that leads to financial losses and job cuts. Shareholders may have a different view, wanting huge rewards from booming profits and share prices – and less worried about risk because limited liability protects them from having to pay out personally for any business losses.

Do accept that risk is not a bad thing – it's simply an inevitable part of making a decision. High risks or unknown risks can be bad – but risk itself is simply inevitable.

Don't assume that reward just means money. Some business owners love what they do – they may love to see new customers eating vegan food or looking fabulous in a wedding dress.

Exam tip: examiners like to see risk weighed up in relation to reward. For example an investor might be happy to take on a high risk if the rewards could be massive (such as the early investor in Facebook who risked $0.5 million and gained $1 billion).

Risk, reward and business activity: 5-step logic chain (for top level response)

Chain 1. When faced with risky business decisions bosses should take their time (1) … taking care to think about the worst that could happen (2) … especially if there's a possibility of losses overwhelming the business finances (3). Then consider the best that could happen, such as providing a new medicine to cure a dangerous disease (4). Business isn't just about profits (5).

Chain 2. Day by day, staff make thousands of decisions in ordinary ways (1) … such as whether to give a disappointed customer his/her money back (2). The risks are greater in a digital world with instant feedback and ratings (3) … which could lead one customer's disappointment to affect hundreds of people's image of the business (4). Good businesses make sure all staff understand this risk. (5)

The use of financial information

What? (Grade 5 basics)

The two most important pieces of financial information are cash flow and profit. Cash flow is often forecast into the future, giving managers a warning if things are about to get difficult. Profit is usually measured looking backwards ('last month's profit was £45,000').

Why? (Grade 6)

Profit is vital because it provides the surplus to fund business growth (reinvested profit). Then the business can avoid using expensive loans or overdrafts. And won't need to sell shares, risking losing control of the business. Cash flow forecasts look into the future, allowing the business to change direction if the financial situation demands it. So profit and cash flow tell a huge amount about past and future.

How? (Grade 7)

Performance can best be measured using comparisons, perhaps over time, e.g. 'profit is up 50% on last year' – showing that the business is moving in the right direction. It can also be tested in relation to rivals, e.g. last year's profit of £120,000 looks disappointing when our rival made £200,000.

So? (Grade 8)

Making good profits isn't just a matter of greed. If your rival keeps making £200,000 to your £120,000, it will be able to advertise more and spend more on its website. If you can't keep up, your profits will be squeezed over time – perhaps eventually forcing you to close down. Profit isn't just a measure of performance, it's a means to survival.

Grade 9

Well-run businesses think in years not months. They plan for the future and for how much capital will be needed to achieve their objectives. Carefully controlled and measured cash flow and profits will help provide the finance necessary. So financial information is important in measuring and understanding business performance and decision making.

> **Do** remember that decision-making is risky, so good financial information can be crucial in avoiding costly mistakes.

> **Don't** forget the importance of non-financial data, such as market share and productivity. Improvements in these figures are likely to feed into higher profits in future. And a worsening in market share or productivity should raise a red flag – things are going wrong.

> **Exam tip**: think about how financial information can help in other departments such as marketing: if profits are falling on a specific brand, surely the marketing has to change.

Financial information: 5-step logic chain (to get to the top level of response)

Chain 1. Break-even analysis shows whether enough product is being sold to make a profit (1) … which may show the need for better sales staff (2) … or for a boost to the motivation of existing staff, so that they sell with more enthusiasm (3). Calculating break-even (fixed costs / contribution per unit) (4) is quicker and more accurate than drawing a break-even chart (5).

Chain 2. Sometimes managers have to decide whether to choose Option A or B (1). The decision can be helped by calculating the profit potential of each option (2). If A is clearly more profitable the decision will go its way (3) … but if the profit calculation shows it's tight between A and B it may be better to make the decision on non-financial grounds (4) …such as which is the more interesting and therefore motivating for staff to produce (5).

Application: the key skill

Problem 1.

Examiners want to do more than test your knowledge of business. They want to know what you can <u>do</u> with that knowledge. Can you weigh up a business problem or opportunity based on a real business situation? That's the skill of application. You applying your mind to a specific business situation – the one the examiner has chosen to write about. The problem is that students skim read the text, rushing to get to the questions.

The Solution

Read the text with care; try to read actively. Think about what's being said or hinted at. Make brief notes in the margin – that's a usefully active thing to do. Don't use a highlighter; that's too passive. And when you've finished reading, jot down what you *feel* about the story. That's important because what you feel is really your judgement. And that links application with another important skill – evaluation. Having read a business story you might feel: 'Risky!' 'Wow, brilliant!' 'Running before they can walk??' or 'Better watch the cash flow'. All these would be likely to lead to fabulous application.

> **Do** jot down points in the margin as you read through the text. Highlighters aren't as effective. And practise short conclusions at the end of the text, based on what you feel, i.e. your gut instinct. And use that to build arguments: 'I think it's too risky because ...'

Problem 2.

Time after time, examiners report that student answers ignore the business context. If the exam material is about *Missguided*, their answers simply mention *Missguided* occasionally. But that's not the point.

The Solution

When reading the short piece about a business, ask yourself: 'what's <u>distinctive</u> or special about this particular company?' Your job is to use that information to answer an exam question such as:

'Analyse two benefits *Missguided* might gain from selling shop franchises.' (6)

Instead of getting lost in explaining the benefits of franchising, a good answer will wrap those benefits around what's special about *Missguided*.

Problem 3.

So how do you decide what's distinctive? The answer is anything that strikes you, i.e. <u>your</u> thoughts are crucial. As long as you can justify why a point is distinctive, the examiner will go along with you.

> **Don't** lose sight of the business story as you work through your answer. On a 9-mark question it's important to make a full reference to the business situation in all 3 sections of your answer: the case for, the counter-argument and the judgement.

The Solution

Read this business start-up story and identify 3 distinctive features:

'Den and girlfriend Pam started PD Ltd. with £15,000 borrowed from a friend and £15,000 from HSBC. Both keen surfers, their plan was to open the first surfing school in the North East, on the coast above Newcastle. They were confident that they could persuade the Geordies to take up surfing, despite the cold weather.'

Now, what did you feel after reading this text? Perhaps 'daft idea' or 'that'll never work' which ideally you'd translate into business-speak: 'Risky!' You might have picked out the risky financing (debt); the importance of the word 'first' – which can be used to build an argument for and an argument against this business idea. You might have picked up on 'keen surfers' – suggesting that their enthusiasm might rub off, giving customers a great experience. The point is it doesn't matter what you select – as long as you pick on one or two distinctive points and build a business argument around them.

> **Exam tip:** be bold not timid. If you think a new product idea seems weak, say so (but you have to explain *why* you say that). Strong opinions matter, though don't ignore the counter-argument. I love Marmite, but I can see why others hate it.

Answers to Maths Questions

1.3.2a) Revenue and costs

Q1a) DF Ltd monthly sales revenue

Quantity x Price = Revenue

800 x £8 = **£6,400**

Q1b) DF Ltd total costs

Total variable costs + Fixed costs = Total costs

(800 units x £2) + £1,500 = **£3,100**

Q2a) Revenue per flight

Number of passengers x Flight price = Revenue per flight

(120 passengers x £50) + (80 x £90) = £6,000 + £7,200 = **£13,200**

Q2b) Total costs

Total variable costs + Fixed costs = Total costs

(200 passengers x £5) + £9,200 = **£10,200**

Q3a) Weekly revenue

(500 cakes x £2) + (600 loaves x £2.50) = **£2,500**

Q3b) Total variable costs + Fixed costs = Total costs

So: (1,100 units x £1) + ? = £2,100

Answer = £2,100 - £1,100 = **£1,000**

Q4a) If Quantity x Price = Revenue

Then Quantity = Revenue / Price

£15,000 / £30 = **500 surfers**

Q4b) If total costs are £12,500 of which £5,000 are fixed, then £7,500 is the total variable cost. So variable costs per hour are £7,500 / 500 surfers = **£15 an hour**

1.3.2b) Profit and Loss

Q1a) BGT Ltd weekly profit/loss

Total Revenue - Total Costs = Profit

(100 x £25) – ([100 x £10] + £900) =

£2,500 - £1,900 = **£600**

Q1b) BGT Ltd weekly profit/loss if sales double

Total Revenue - Total Costs = Profit

(200 x £25) – ([200 x £10] + £900) =

£5,000 - £2,900 = **£2,100**

Do make sure to set out the formula you're using to answer maths questions. It helps the examiner, but much more importantly it helps you structure your answer. That makes mistakes much less likely.

Don't forget that fixed costs can change. Rents can rise and interest rates can rise or fall. The thing about fixed costs is they're fixed in relation to output.

Exam tip: maths questions will be 10% of the marks on each exam paper. But they're a hugely important 10%. If you're good at them, 10/10 is a serious possibility. While others will be getting 0/10. That makes maths questions a big swing factor in getting grades.

Answers to Maths Questions

Q2. A clothes store's weekly profit

Revenue: (400 × £15) + (250 × £4) = £7,000

Variable costs (400 × £4) + (250 × £2) = £2,100

Profit = £7,000 − (£2,100 + £1,200) = **£3,700**

> **Don't** panic if OCR has forced you to calculate revenue or costs for two products. The principles remain exactly the same.

Q3. The farmer's strawberries

3a) Weekly total costs: (5,000 kilos × £0.40p = £2,000) + £6,500 = **£8,500**

3b) Weekly profit = £10,000 - £8,500 = **£1,500**

Q4a) Number of surfers = £24,000 / £30 = **800 surfers**

Q4b) Profit = Revenue £24,000 − Total costs £15,000 = **£9,000**

Q4c) New profit = Revenue £36,000 − (£16,000 variable + £7,000 fixed) = **£13,000 profit**

1.3.3 Cash Flow

1. BVK Ltd

If the net cash flow this month is £33,000 - £30,000 = +£3,000 …

… and there's a closing balance of +£10,000

… then the month's opening balance must have been **+£7,000**

2a) Clothing business cash flow

a) £300

b) £3,300

c) £7,000

d) -£3,000

e) -£3,900

> **Don't** be surprised if you have to complete a cash flow table. Examiners love it because it's so easy to mark!

2b) It's only possible if the business has a big enough overdraft agreed with the bank.

3. Might be incorrect because the sales forecast proved to be wrong – which is almost inevitable for a new business. However much was spent on market research, you could never be certain about the number of customers for a new business.

Could also be incorrect because of competitors' responses to your opening. In such a cutthroat sector as pizza delivery (with huge rivals such as Domino's) unexpectedly sharp price cutting by rivals may dent your customer numbers (and threaten your ability to survive the difficult early months)

> **Exam tip:** even with finance questions remember the business context. Here, it's easy to make references to the pizza market.